MEDIA TODAY

Interpreting Newspapers, Magazines, Radio, TV, Movies and the Internet

D. Addison

GLOBE FEARON
EDUCATIONAL PUBLISHER
A Division of Simon & Schuster
Upper Saddle River, New Jersey

Director of Editorial and Marketing: Nancy Surridge
Project Editor: Amy Jolin
Editorial Development: Curriculum Concepts Inc.
Production Editor: John Roberts
Art Director: Pat Smythe
Interior Design and
    Electronic Page Production: Margarita T. Giammanco
Interior Illustrations: Donna Nettis, Melanie Hope Greenberg, Jane Caminos, Circa 86
Cover Design: Oh! Jackie, Inc.
Cover Illustration: Salem Krieger

Photo Credits:

1, The Bettmann Archive; Photofest. 2, The Bettmann Archive; Wernher Krutein/Liaison International. 4, The Bettmann Archive. 36, Photofest; Tony Freeman, Photo Edit; The Bettmann Archive. 45, Reuters/Bettmann. 64, The Bettmann Archive. 66, The Bettmann Archive; AP Wide World Photos; UPI/Bettmann; The Library of Congress. 68, UPI/Bettmann. 71, Wide World Photos. 76, Wide World Photos. 82, Photofest. 99, Photofest; Courtesy of MTV. 100, Gamma Liaison. 103, Courtesy of Coca-Cola, Liaison International. 104, Gamma Liaison Network; Gamma Liaison. 105, Gamma Liaison Network. 109, Photofest. 110, Photofest. 115, Photofest. 120 Photofest. 127, Courtesy of ENIAC; Liaison International; Fredrik D. Bodin/Stock Boston; Wernher Krutein; Liaison International.

CONTENTS

INTRODUCTION

THE POWER OF THE MEDIA

Suppose you wanted to give someone a message. How many ways of communicating can you think of? You could speak to the person face to face. You could make a phone call. You could write a letter. If you have a computer, you could send electronic "mail."

Now suppose you wanted to communicate with more than one person. How could you send your message to a large number of people at the same time? You could shout from a rooftop. You could post a sign. You could send out many copies of the same letter.

Shouting, posting signs, and writing letters are all means of communication. You could reach dozens, even hundreds, of people by these means. But what if you wanted to communicate with thousands or millions of people? That would be **mass communication**. You would be communicating with a **mass**, or large number, of people.

Technology has made mass communication possible. Thanks to inventions like the printing press and the microchip, we can communicate with huge numbers of people at one time. Newspapers and magazines communicate through printed words and pictures. Radio uses sound to communicate. Television and movies communicate through sound and moving pictures.

What Are Mass Media?

Each method of communication is a **medium**. The plural of *medium* is **media**. Media that communicate with a mass of people are called **mass media**. Mass media include:

newspapers	movies
magazines	radio
books	recordings
television	computers

These media can serve different purposes. They can convey information. They can

1

entertain you. They can try to persuade you to think or act a certain way. Sometimes they can serve two or even three purposes at once.

For example, recall a TV or radio talk show that you enjoyed. Think carefully. Did the show inform you? Entertain you? Persuade you? What do you think was the main purpose of the show?

Are You Media-Wise?

The mass media are powerful. People tend to believe what they read on the printed page or see on the screen. However, the media do not always present a fair or complete picture. For this reason, people must think carefully about messages that the media send. They need to evaluate what they see and hear. They must separate fact from opinion. They must learn to tell the difference between information and entertainment. In other words, people must become media-*wise*.

Media-wise readers, viewers, and listeners ask questions. They do not simply accept what the media presents. They look for false or misleading ideas. They watch for hidden messages. They consider all sides of an issue before forming an opinion.

The Business of Advertising

Advertising plays a big part in the media. Companies pay to run ads in newspapers and magazines. They pay to air commercials on TV and radio. These ads and commercials share one purpose. They want to persuade you to buy products. The more you buy, the more money advertisers make.   Being media-wise means recognizing the purpose— and the power—of advertising.

The money that companies pay to advertise their products, keeps the media in business. But advertising money can influence the media. Here is an example. A magazine article includes special praise for the DZS Clothing Company. DZS advertises in the magazine. The magazine publisher knows that favorable mention will please DZS. DZS will then be likely to buy more ad space. How might DZS react if the magazine criticized the company?

Sometimes the influence of advertising is even more subtle. Have you ever seen an actor in a TV show or movie use a familiar product? It is no accident that the actor uses that particular brand. The company that makes the product has paid to have it shown on your TV screen. The company knows that many people will buy a product the actor "likes". Media-wise viewers know that this is a form of advertising.

Zeroing in on the Media

You have probably heard the word **literacy** many times. It means the ability to read and write. Today the word is also used another way. People speak of the need for **media literacy**. Media literacy is just another term for being media-wise. Someone who is **media-literate** understands media methods. He or she is not misled by media messages.

Media literacy is important because the mass media affect everyone. People read newspapers and magazines. They listen to radio. They use computers. And, of course, people watch TV. These media flood us with information and images. They color our views. They influence our actions.

Around the country, there is a growing call for media literacy. More and more schools are teaching students how to cope with the power of the media. Students are learning to be media-wise readers, viewers, and listeners. Here are some of the ideas they are exploring. Take a moment to think about each one.

- The media entertain and teach us. But the media can also mislead us.
- The media try to be fair. Yet, the media do not always treat all people equally.
- The media may show the truth. But the media may also create false images.

Some are obvious, others are not.
- We can learn about almost any subject from the media. But sometimes the media blur the lines between advice, information, and advertisement.
- As the media inform us, they may also try to persuade us.
- Advertisers use various methods to sell their products. Some methods influence us without our knowledge.

In this book, you will examine these ideas and many others. You will explore and clarify your views of the media. You will sharpen your ability to judge messages that the media send.

Welcome to Media Today

This book has four parts. Part 1 focuses on newspapers and magazines. Part 2 deals with audio media: radio and recordings. Part 3 examines television and the movies. Part 4 explores computer-based media.

In each part, you will learn about the power of the media. You will see how and why people use different media to communicate. Questions and activities throughout the book will give you a chance to share ideas and let you apply what you learn.

Learning about the media does not end in the classroom. Use your knowledge to help you think about media messages you receive each day. Ask yourself questions: *Does this article tell the whole story? Is this TV show painting a true picture? Can I trust this speaker's words?*

The world is always changing. Each day brings new information. If you are media-wise, you can sort through this information. You can analyze what you see and hear. You can make up your own mind about key issues. Most importantly, you can think for yourself.

PART 1

FOCUS ON NEWSPAPERS AND MAGAZINES

People. Places. Dates. Events.

Every day we face a flood of information. Newspapers and magazines are two sources that give us information and also help us understand it.

Newspapers tell us what is happening. They report the news around the world and across the street. They show us photos. They describe events.

Magazines inform us, too. Through magazines, we share other people's knowledge. We also learn from other people's experience. We find facts in magazines that we cannot find in newspapers.

Together, these two forms of **print media** make us wiser. They teach us about our world. They help us look at issues from different points of view. They help us form opinions.

Readers and Topics Most adults in the United States read a daily newspaper. Most also read one or more magazines each month. In our country, eleven newspapers sell more than a half million copies *per day*. Twenty magazines sell over three million copies *per issue*.

Newspapers and magazines offer something for everyone. Readers can find articles on any topic in the world.

Some magazines are written for a general audience. There are also magazines written especially for women, for men, for teens, and for children. There are articles for readers who are experts. There are articles for beginners.

Advertising Advertising plays a very important role in keeping newspapers and magazines in business. About two-thirds of the cost of producing newspapers and magazines is paid for by advertisements, or ads.

Ads take up about 60 percent of the space in newspapers. In fact, in newspapers, ads are placed *first*. The articles fill the leftover space.

Most magazines reach a wider audience than newspapers because they are published across the nation. Through magazines, advertisers can sell their products nationally.

Magazine ads can be aimed at certain readers. They can reach those who are most likely to buy certain products. For example, a company that makes tennis rackets advertises in a tennis magazine.

Without the money from ads, publishers could not stay in business. This gives advertisers some power over what is printed. They can influence which articles are printed next to their ad.

Impact Newspapers and magazines provide more facts than a brief TV or radio show because there is more room for more information. Newspapers and magazines let readers read at their own pace. They also allow readers to choose exactly what they want to read about.

Since newspapers are printed every day people read them to learn about current events. They learn about events around the world, in their state, and in their community.

Magazines are printed less often than newspapers. They explore subjects in depth. There are magazines in print on almost any subject you are interested in.

With all their information, newspapers and magazines shape people's ideas. They provide facts that people need to form opinions. They educate and guide readers.

Issues Many people criticize newspapers. Some people object to the shocking stories about crime and violence. They think newspapers highlight these stories to sell more copies. Some critics claim that stories are biased. Biased stories may mislead readers since they present only one side of the issue.

Magazines have critics, too. Sometimes articles mix fact and opinion, and readers cannot tell which is which. Some critics complain that advertisers have too much power. Magazines listen closely to what advertisers think because they do not want to lose ad money.

People also argue over what readers should be protected from.

In Part 1, you will explore these issues. Think carefully about each one. What is your opinion?

Long before radio and TV, newspapers reported the events of the day. In fact, the first daily paper was published in Rome in 59 B.C.

Today, about 1,600 newspapers are published each day in the United States. About 7,500 other papers appear less often. Some are published weekly. Others are published monthly.

Some newspapers, such as the *Wall Street Journal* and *USA Today*, are sold nationally and even outside the country. Other papers are published only in one state, city, or town.

What News Do Papers Cover?

Newspaper articles describe events in the world around us. **International news** is about events in other nations. An earthquake in Japan or a war in the Middle East is international news. **National news** is about events in our own country. A presidential election is national news.

Regional news relates to a smaller area. For example, a regional paper may highlight events in one state. **Local news** focuses on a county or town. For example, voters read local news to learn who is running for mayor. Local news also includes the special events of the local area, such as parades and concerts.

▶ A newspaper's name may tell where the paper is published and the area it serves. For example, the *Sacramento Union* is published in Sacramento, California.

▶ Some newspapers publish several different editions. Each edition covers local news for a certain area.

News events often fall into more than one category. The 1995 bombing of a federal building was local news in Oklahoma City. But the event was important enough to be front-page news across the nation.

Kinds of Newspapers

Newspapers differ in many ways. Some papers balance international, national, and local news. Others may only report on business or science news. Others have mostly stories about the political side of the news. Some papers have short articles, bold headlines, and many photos. Others have longer articles, smaller headlines, and fewer photos. Whether you are interested in crime, antiques, or movie stars, there is a newspaper for you.

Much of the news in daily papers also appears in TV and radio reports and in news magazines. Weekly papers, such as those in small towns, report the news that readers cannot easily find elsewhere. For example, people read town papers to find out about local sports. Some papers have an even narrower focus. A high school paper covers school events.

◄ Publishers try to include articles that appeal to their specific readers. For example, a paper serving an area with many Hispanic readers will run stories about Hispanic cultural events.

Who Publishes the News?

The number of people needed to publish a newspaper varies. A large paper may employ more than eighty full-time workers and many part-timers. A small paper may have only a few workers.

A newspaper staff includes reporters, editors, writers, photographers, and artists. Other people work to produce and print the final newspaper pages. There is also a team of workers that sells ad space.

◄ A daily paper may earn 70 to 80 percent of its money from advertising.

Newspapers and Advertising

Does it seem that some newspapers have as many ads as articles? Many papers do. In fact, a daily paper uses more than half of its space for advertising. This is because most newspaper publishers do not make a profit selling papers. They make money by selling ad space. Without ads, few daily papers could survive.

◄ Take a close look at a daily newspaper. Which ads are on the same page as articles? Which ads fill whole pages? Which ads are at the back of the paper?

Lesson 1
Hard News and Soft News

Reading a newspaper is different from reading a book. When you read a book, you read every page. Few people read every page of a newspaper. They only read the articles that interest them.

Newspapers organize their content to help readers find what they want. Similar stories are grouped into sections. Here are some typical sections in a daily newspaper:

International news	National news
Local news	Business
Entertainment	Sports
Editorial	Classified advertisements

Newspapers contain hard news and soft news. **Hard news** is a factual account of an important event. **Soft news** includes stories that are interesting, but less important than hard news. Soft news is often background information. A report of a tornado striking a town is hard news. An interview with someone who saw the tornado is soft news. Articles in which writers express their opinions are soft news, too. Editorials and movie reviews are examples.

Here are some other examples of hard and soft news:

Hard News	**Soft News**
speech by the President	new hair styles
medical breakthrough	restaurant review
election results	interview with a rap singer
bank robbery	holiday parade
business statistics	advice column
weather information	popularity of soccer

Newspapers generally put the most important stories on the front page. However, some papers put eye-catching stories on the front page, even if they are not major news. The publishers hope to grab people's attention and sell more papers. What kind of newspaper headlines and photos attract your attention?

Most papers contain more soft news than hard news. A popular kind of soft news is the **human-interest story**. Human-interest stories deal with the human side of the news. Often they describe unusual events. A story may tell how a teen saved her brother. Another story may tell how a cat stowed away on a plane. Why do you think people enjoy reading human-interest stories?

When you read a book, you know what to expect. If the book is a novel, the content is fiction. If the book is nonfiction, the content is fact. But newspapers mix content. Some articles simply report information. Other articles mix facts with the writer's thoughts and feelings.

It is important to learn how to read newspaper articles critically. By analyzing what you read, you should be able to tell the difference between fact and opinion. Ask yourself if the article contains hard news or soft news. Does the writer state facts or opinions? Does the article favor one viewpoint over another? Reading critically will help you understand and evaluate information.

Look through the next two articles then answer the following four questions on a separate sheet.

THE LANGUAGE OF THINKING

Critical readers separate facts from opinions. A **fact** is information that can be proved to be true. "The police arrested a suspect," is a statement of fact. An **opinion** is a belief based on a person's judgment. "I think the police probably arrested the wrong man," is an opinion. Opinions are usually based on facts. However, an opinion based on facts is still just an opinion until it can be proved.

Head Zup Banned From Music Fest

The city Commissioner's office has canceled the tour of the most popularly requested punk rock group among teens aged 13 to 18.

Head Zup has attracted much attention over the past year as their popularity and record sales have skyrocketed. School and parent organizations object to lyrics which are profane and lude. Such lyrics have led to the arrest of the lead singer 4 times during the last 12 months.

The group had scheduled a performance during the summer music festival. After loud objections from parents and schools, their performance has been canceled from the roster just one month before the festival is to begin.

Reaction to the Commissioner's decision has been unanimously positive.

Japan Sets Sights on Moon and Mars

The late 1990's could see Japan send a space craft to the Moon and to Mars.

The goal of the lunar mission is to learn more about the interior of the Moon. The spacecraft will launch 3 probes into the Moon's surface. They will each plunge 3 to 10 feet into moon dust. The probes will measure any moonquakes, as well as changes in the Moon's surface temperature.

The mission to Mars will focus on learning about the Martian atmosphere. A spacecraft will orbit the planet very close to the surface. It will use a camera to study Martian weather and surface features.

9

To **imply** something means to say it indirectly. When writers imply a judgment, they give an opinion without actually stating it. Here is an example from a sports article: "Surprisingly, the Yankees are still clinging to second place in the standings." What judgment does this writer imply? Does the writer think the Yankees will stay in second place? What words tell you what the writer is really thinking?

Headlines can imply judgment, too. Compare the following two headlines:

CITIZENS OBJECT TO MAYOR'S PLAN

ANGRY MOB SHOUTS DOWN MAYOR

Which headline sounds more negative? What words make it sound more negative?

1. What is the main idea of the article?

2. Does the article present facts, opinions, or a mixture of both? Support your answer with examples.

3. Does the article make or imply a judgment? Explain.

4. What is the article's purpose: to inform you, entertain you, or convince you of something? Give reasons for your answer.

   Find three articles that interest you. Choose articles from different sections of the paper. Read each article critically. Answer the same questions from the previous exercise.

Lesson 2
Facts or Feelings?

Not all newspapers have the same style. **Mainstream newspapers** take a serious, low-key approach to the news. They report facts, not feelings. **Tabloid newspapers** are more dramatic. Tabloid pages have more photos and use bigger print. Bold headlines scream at the reader. Tabloid stories are shorter than stories in mainstream papers. Often they focus on sensational or shocking news.

The publishers of mainstream and tabloid papers have a common goal. They both want to sell newspapers. Since many readers enjoy the breezy style of tabloids, many mainstream newspapers are beginning to imitate them.

Many mainstream newspapers are reporting more soft news. They include short articles written in a chatty style. They run stories about the personal lives of famous people. They use bigger headlines and more photos.

Some critics object to such changes in the mainstream papers. They say that tabloid news makes readers feel instead of think. They believe that newspapers should focus on important topics. These critics think the purpose of a newspaper is to inform readers, not entertain them.

Compare the following two article excerpts. Both articles are about the same subject but are written very differently. The article on the left is from a mainstream paper. The article on the right is from a tabloid.

"Superman" Actor Injured in Fall

Actor Christopher Reeve was seriously injured yesterday when he fell from his horse during a riding competition in Virginia. The accident occurred when Reeve's horse refused to jump a three-foot fence. The horse stopped short, throwing Reeve headfirst over the fence.

The 42-year-old actor was rushed to the hospital. Doctors report that neck fractures have injured Reeve's spinal cord. He is paralyzed and can breathe only with the aid of a respirator.

Reeve is best known for playing the role of Superman in four movies. He has also appeared in more than a dozen other films.

"MAN OF STEEL" BREAKS NECK
May Never Walk Again

♦ ♦ ♦

A horse did what the bad guys never could. It stopped Superman.

Christopher Reeve once flew through the air as a comic-book superhero in the movies. Now the popular actor is lying paralyzed in a Virginia hospital. His neck is broken, and he needs a machine to breathe.

Reeve, 42, was hurled over a fence during a riding competition. Horrified witnesses saw him crash to the ground headfirst. The fall left him unconscious, with two smashed bones in his neck.

"This is a dreadful injury," a nurse commented. "To see him lying there ...it's a tragedy. The man can't move. He can't take a breath on his own. He can't even talk. He can only mouth words. It breaks my heart."

THE LANGUAGE OF THINKING

Tone and style refer to how an article is written. **Tone** is the way a writer expresses a feeling. For example, an article that sounds "chatty" has a friendly tone. News articles in mainstream papers generally have a more formal tone than those in tabloids. **Style** is the way a writer puts ideas into words. For example, some writers use long sentences and fancy words. Others use short sentences and simple words.

Answer the following questions about the two articles.

1. What facts appear in both articles?

_____

_____

2. How would you describe the tone and style of each article?
   MAINSTREAM ARTICLE

_____

   TABLOID ARTICLE

_____

3. Both articles report the same news event. However, the writers use different words and organize facts differently. Explain the differences, and give examples.

_____

_____

4. Which article was meant to make you "feel" more? How do you know?

_____

_____

5. How does each headline help to set a different tone?

_____

_____

6. Each article begins very differently. How does this difference affect the tone?

_____

_____

DISCUSSION

• •

Do some newspapers go too far? Should there be a limit on what newspapers can report? How do you feel about each of the following questions?

- Should news stories cover the private lives of people in the news? For example, do reporters have the right to write about a senator's marriage?
- Should newspapers describe the bloody details of awful crimes? Should they include photos of the victims?
- Should newspapers publish the names of children under 18 who are accused of a crime?

MEDIA WISE

People often argue about what newspapers should or should not be allowed to print. Some people believe that certain material should be **censored**—kept away from the public. For example, you may agree that pornographic pictures do not belong in a newspaper. But is it all right to publish a photo of a topless actress on a beach?

Other questions of censorship are even harder to answer. Should a newspaper be allowed to tell how a criminal made a bomb? Should a newspaper reveal government secrets? How much does the public have a right to know?

Next time you read a news article, ask yourself what facts or details the writer has left out—and why.

Lesson 3
Articles That Persuade

Editorials and columns can have great influence. For example, they play a key role in political campaigns. Voters often do not understand the issues of a campaign. Editorials and columns discuss the issues and compare candidates.

The purpose of a newspaper is to report the news. But many readers want more than facts. They want opinions. They want to know what other people think about important issues.

Editorials and columns are articles in which people give their opinions. An **editorial** states the opinion of a newspaper editor or owner. A **column** gives the views of a writer, or **columnist**.

Writers of editorials and columns try to persuade readers. They want readers to agree with their views. The writers support their ideas with facts. However, sometimes they exaggerate the facts. Other times they make scary claims without supporting facts. They may try to mislead the reader. Often the writers try to convince readers that there is only one way to view an issue.

By reading other people's opinions, you can better understand issues. Then you can make your own judgments. But remember that editorials and columns may present only one viewpoint. Before you make a judgment, learn the *opposing* point of view, too.

Read the following editorial. What are the writer's beliefs? How does the writer try to persuade you?

Most newspapers have an **op-ed page**. This page usually appears opposite the page with the editorials. The op-ed page has columns, articles, and sometimes cartoons. On this page, people express their views on various subjects. The op-ed page also includes letters written by readers. How can reading both the editorial page and the op-ed page give you a balanced view of issues?

"PEOPLE POLLUTION" IN OUR NATIONAL PARKS

WE ARE RUINING OUR NATIONAL parks. Their quiet beauty is being killed by people pollution.

Consider the Grand Canyon. It's probably our finest park. Nearly 5 *million* tourists overran the canyon in 1994. This summer, more than 25,000 people will flood the park *daily*.

These crowds trample everything in their path. They throw garbage everywhere. The rumbling motors of cars and campers poison the air and shatter the silence. Sightseeing planes and helicopters add to the confusion.

It's time to stop the madness. It's time to save the Grand Canyon and our other parks.

Limit the number of people allowed to visit. Ban motor vehicles. Ban planes. Ban helicopters. Slap heavy fines on people who litter. Hire more rangers to patrol the parks.

Act now, before our national parks become a national disgrace.

Now answer the following questions to help you evaluate the editorial.

1. Does the author convince you that there is a problem?

_____

_____

2. Are the facts in the article accurate and believable?

_____

_____

3. Does the author offer reasonable solutions to the problem?

_____

_____

4. Suppose this were a news article. Would the information be presented in the same way? Explain.

_____

_____

5. The writer uses words like *killed*, *poison*, and *madness*. What feeling does the writer want to create by using such words?

_____

_____

6. What arguments might someone with an opposing viewpoint offer?

_____

_____

7. Do you think the editorial presents a fair view of the issue? Why or why not?

_____

_____

THE LANGUAGE OF THINKING

When you **evaluate** something, you judge its worth or value. When you evaluate an article that expresses a point of view, examine it critically. Which statements contain facts? Which are opinions? Has the writer omitted important information? Do the writer's arguments make sense? Is the conclusion logical? Answers to such questions will help you weigh the article's value.

Comparing Newspapers

In this activity, you will use what you have learned to examine and compare two newspapers. Work with a small group of classmates. Follow these steps:

- Obtain two different newspapers that are published in your state or community.
- Examine the contents of both papers. Discuss your observations with group members.
- Discuss each of the following questions. Then write your answer.

1. Which paper has more international and national news?

   _____

2. Which paper has more local news?

   _____

3. Do both papers have a balance of hard news and soft news? Explain your answer.

   _____

4. Which paper has bolder headlines and more pictures?

   _____

5. Do you consider each paper a mainstream newspaper or a tabloid? Why?

   _____

Now summarize your comparisons by answering the following questions on a separate piece of paper.

6. List six ways that the papers are alike.

7. List six ways that the papers are different.

8. Which paper do you prefer? Give six reasons why.

Unit Test

Checking What You Have Learned

1. You should always ask yourself which statements in a newspaper article are fact and which are opinion. State whether you agree or disagree with this statement. Explain.

   _____

   _____

2. Put an X next to the statement that is true. Explain your choice on the lines provided.

   ❏ You can easily tell if an article comes from a mainstream paper or a tabloid.

   ❏ Some articles in mainstream papers resemble tabloid articles.

   _____

   _____

3. Why is it important to know whether an article's purpose is to inform you, entertain you, or convince you of something? Give examples to support your answer.

   _____

   _____

4. How can reading several editorials and columns about the same issue help you form an opinion about that issue? Write your anwer on a separate sheet of paper.

Checking How You Learned

Use the following questions to evaluate your performance in this unit.
- What did you learn about differences between hard news and soft news?
- What did you learn about similarities and differences between mainstream and tabloid newspapers?
- How can separating fact from opinion help you evaluate what you read?

UNIT 2 Magazines: Facts, Views, and Fun

Do you read *Mad Magazine*? How about *'Teen* or *Sports Illustrated*? If so, you are not alone. Each of these magazines has a million or more readers. Some magazines have many times that number. *Reader's Digest* has more than 16 million readers.

About 12,000 different magazines are published in the United States. Some are **general interest magazines**. General interest magazines try to appeal to many different readers. The articles and features offer something for everyone. *Reader's Digest, Newsweek,* and *People* are general interest magazines.

Nine out of ten magazines are **special interest magazines**. Special interest magazines are aimed only at certain readers. For example, *YM* and *Sassy* are written for female teens. *Cat Fancy* is written for cat lovers. *PC Computing* is for computer users. Many special interest magazines aim at *very* specific audiences. Who do you think reads the following magazines?

Bicycling	*Parents Magazine*	*Opinion World*
Firehouse Magazine	*Stamp Collector*	*Backpacker*

▶ As TV became popular, many famous weekly general interest magazines went out of business. A few have come back as monthly magazines. For instance, *Life* first appeared as a weekly in 1936. It stopped publication in 1972. In 1978, it returned as a monthly.

Why are there so many more special interest magazines than general interest magazines? There are two reasons. The first is television. Magazines aimed at a general audience find it hard to compete with TV. Television offers more general information and entertainment than any magazine can. More people will watch TV rather than read a magazine.

On the other hand, television offers little of the specific information found in special interest magazines. Dentists will not learn about dental products from TV. Instead, they read *Dental Economics*.

The second reason why there are so many more special interest magazines is advertising. Like newspapers, magazines earn most of

18

their money through advertising. If you have a product to sell, you want to be sure the people who might buy your product see your ads. Suppose that you sell bowling equipment. Would you rather advertise in a general interest magazine or in *Bowling* magazine? Magazines aimed at specific readers create a direct line for advertisers. Bowlers and nonbowlers read general interest magazines. Only bowlers read *Bowling*.

Why People Read Magazines

Most magazine articles provide information. News magazines focus on current events. Sports magazines provide information about one sport or many. Fashion magazines discuss the latest styles.

Some articles are written to help readers. A computer magazine compares different software. A consumer magazine offers shopping advice. A gardening magazine gives tips for plant care.

Many magazines are meant to entertain. *Mad* is a humor magazine. *Soap Opera Digest* covers soap operas and their stars. *Us* focuses on famous people.

Many magazines also contain editorials and columns, just like those in newspapers. (Look back at Lesson 3 of Unit 1.) These articles clearly express an opinion. But some articles that are not editorials or columns also state an opinion.

Magazine articles often present information from one writer's viewpoint. A veterinarian may express views about how to train a puppy. A teen magazine may have an article about sports equipment. The article may name certain products. Are these the "best" products? Maybe, maybe not.

Most magazines contain a mixture of articles. For example, a magazine for parents may have articles about school and Little League. The magazine may also have a family's story of moving to another state. There may also be product reviews and an "ask-the-doctor" column. By offering such variety, the magazine hopes to interest many readers.

Who Writes Magazine Articles?

Some magazines have full-time writers on staff. But most magazine articles are written by **freelance writers**, or **freelancers**. Freelancers do not work for only one magazine. They sell articles to different magazines.

◀ The leading general interest magazines reach millions of readers. For this reason, they charge high prices for advertising space. Ads in special interest magazines cost much less. These magazines have fewer readers, but they are *interested* readers. The best place to advertise depends on the product. Suppose you owned a chain of fast-food restaurants. Would you advertise in a general or special interest magazine? Why?

◀ Sometimes advertised products also appear in a magazine's articles or photos. Why might a magazine favor the products of its advertisers?

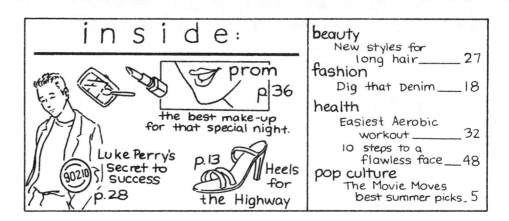

inside:

prom p.36

the best make-up for that special night.

Luke Perry's Secret to Success p.28

p.13 Heels for the Highway

▶ A magazine's **editor** chooses articles for the magazine. The editor decides what issues are most important for the magazine to cover. The editor also determines in what order the articles will appear.

▶ The writer of a magazine article may know a great deal about the subject. The person may even be an expert in the field. Or, the writer may have only limited knowledge. As you read an article, see if you can figure out what qualified the person to write it. Is the person writing from experience?

A freelancer may suggest an article idea to the magazine editor. Or, an editor may ask a writer to write a specific article. Usually the writer must do research. Some articles require the writer to interview one or more people.

Freelancers are paid for each article they sell. A magazine with millions of readers may pay hundreds or thousands of dollars for an article. A special interest magazine with far fewer readers may pay less than fifty dollars.

The Power of Magazines

Magazines influence readers in many ways. Articles that give an opinion can persuade readers to share that opinion. Advice columns tell readers to act a certain way. Fashion tips and clothing ads tell readers how to dress.

Many articles have a friendly, informal tone. This encourages readers to believe what they read.

The influence of a magazine can be subtle. Writers often imply an opinion rather than state it. Photographs highlight certain people or products. These are the people or products the reader will remember. The content of a magazine also lets you know which topics are presently "hot" and which are not.

Lesson 1
Planning the Articles

Pretend you are a magazine editor. You have to pick articles for the next issue. How will you choose?

First, think about your readers. How old are they? Are they mostly male or female? Then think about why they read your magazine. Do they want information? Advice? Entertainment? Gossip?

Next, consider the time of year. Is this a summer issue? If so, you may want to have an article on water sports. For winter, you may want an article on snowstorms. Choose articles that apply to the season

Finally, consider the advertising. Companies pay to place their ads in your magazine. Your magazine needs this money to survive. You want to keep the advertisers happy. To do this, you need articles that work well with the ads. For example, a company that advertises clothes likes fashion articles. If an article mentions their products, so much the better. Maybe a photo can even show their clothes.

Look at the following article excerpt. It comes from a magazine aimed at teens. The magazine carries many ads. Two of its advertisers are Power-Up! skates and STAR-1 clothing.

Magazines do research to learn about their readers. They send out surveys. They talk to readers. They study where their magazine sells well or poorly. Such research is called **demographics**. How can demographics help a magazine publisher? Why are demographics important to advertisers?

The more money an advertiser spends, the more power it has. Some big advertisers tell magazines where to place their ads. For example, a food company might require that its pudding ad be placed next to a "positive" article. It might also have to be at least six pages away from other pudding ads. A magazine would have to comply. If not, it would lose the food company's business.

Writers who are not experts get information from other sources. This writer quotes a skating champion. Quoted sources show that a writer has done research. Books and newspapers are other sources writers quote.

GET IN - LINE for ACTION!

By Lisa Reeves

Are you a couch potato? Is your idea of exercise lifting a fork? Well, get up and get skating!

In-line skating is hot. You can burn calories and have a blast, too. "This sport gets you in shape fast," says Doron Steger, a New Jersey skating champion. "Athletes use it to train."

In-line skates are a cross between roller skates and hockey skates. You have a wide choice of brands. "I like Power-Up! skates," says Steger. "They're smooth and well-balanced."

Remember to protect yourself. Wear a helmet and wrist guards. You'll also need elbow and knee pads. Then you're ready to fly!

Answer the following questions about the article.

1. What is the purpose of the article?

   _____

2. Why is this a good article for the magazine?

   _____

3. What facts does the article contain? What opinions?

   FACTS:

   _____

   OPINIONS:

   _____

4. Where do you think the writer got her information?

   _____

5. Why do you think the article mentions Power-Up! skates?

   _____

6. Why do you think the girl in the photo is wearing a STAR-1 shirt?

   _____

7. Why might this article make readers more likely to buy Power-Up! skates and STAR-1 clothing?

   _____

DISCUSSION

••

In 1970, cigarette ads were banned from TV and radio. Therefore tobacco companies ran more ads in magazines.

Many tobacco companies are part of larger companies that make many products. Large companies spend a lot of money on ads. Magazines with cigarette ads usually will not write about the dangers of smoking. They do not want to lose the ad money.

What do you think about this? Is this fair to readers?

Lesson 2
Looking Closely at Magazines

Magazine publishing is hard work. A magazine must give its readers what they want. If it does, the magazine will sell well, companies will pay to advertise, and the magazine will succeed. If it does not, the magazine will not sell. Advertisers will go elsewhere. The magazine will fail.

Obtain two different magazines. Choose at least one that you have never read. Check your library for new magazines.

Read each magazine for about thirty minutes. Then complete the following chart.

Each magazine tries to appeal to certain readers. These readers are its **target audience**. Who is the target audience for *TV Guide?* Who is the target audience for *Surfer?* Which audience do you think is larger? Why?

	MAGAZINE #1	MAGAZINE #2
NAME	_____	_____
HOW OFTEN PUBLISHED	_____	_____
TARGET AUDIENCE (be specific)	_____	_____
	_____	_____
PURPOSE (inform, entertain, other)	_____	_____
NUMBER OF PAGES	_____	_____
ADS (many / some / few)	_____	_____
PHOTOS (many / some / few)	_____	_____
SPECIAL FEATURES	_____	_____
	_____	_____

Answer these questions about the magazines.

1. list six clues that helped you identify the target audience?

   MAGAZINE 1

   _____

   _____

   MAGAZINE 2

   _____

   _____

2. How does the magazine try to appeal to its audience?

   MAGAZINE 1

   _____

   _____

   MAGAZINE 2

   _____

   _____

3. What kinds of ads does the magazine contain?

   MAGAZINE 1

   _____

   _____

   MAGAZINE 2

   _____

   _____

4. Whom are the ads aimed at? How do you know?

   MAGAZINE 1

   _____

   _____

   MAGAZINE 2

   _____

   _____

5. Do the articles and ads work well together? Explain.

   MAGAZINE 1

   _____

   _____

   MAGAZINE 2

   _____

   _____

6. How are the magazines alike? Think about content and format.

   _____

   _____

7. How do the magazines differ?

   _____

   _____

Your Opinion

   Which magazine do you like better? Why?

   _____

   _____

   _____

   _____

To **analyze** something, means to examine it very closely. You study each part. You consider how the parts work together.

Try to analyze magazine articles in order to understand them better. A magazine article may have many parts. There may be facts and numbers. There may be quotations. There may be charts and pictures.

Think about the parts. How does each one add to the whole?

Critical readers analyze what they read. They think about what writers say and how they say it. They try to distinguish facts from opinions. They look for feelings behind the words. They ask questions. What is the writer's point of view? What has the writer assumed? Has the writer assumed correctly?

Read the following article excerpt. It comes from a general interest magazine.

TEENS ARE RISKING THEIR LIVES
by Michael Adams

Huffing—The word sounds harmless. It reminds you of the big, bad wolf: "I'll huff and I'll puff. . ."

But today the word has a new meaning. And it's anything but harmless.

"Huffing" means breathing in chemical fumes to get high. The fumes come from household products you can buy at the store. These products are cheap and legal. They're also very dangerous.

Huffing has killed thousands of people. Some die after months of chemical abuse. Others die the first time they huff. In fact, a British study found that three out of ten teens die the first time they try huffing.

Answer the following questions about the article.

1. What is the main idea of the article?

   _____

   _____

2. Does the article consist mainly of fact or opinion? Give examples.

   _____

   _____

3. How does the writer show his feelings about the topic?

   _____

   _____

4. How might the article affect teens? How might it affect their parents?

   _____

   _____

5. What is the article's purpose? Does the writer accomplish this purpose? Explain.

   _____

   _____

6. The writer seems to imply that most teens abuse chemicals. Is this fair? Explain.

   _____

   _____

7. Suppose the writer had been a teen. How might the article have been written differently?

   _____

   _____

MEDIA WISE

Writers try to make their writing personal. They write about people, not just facts. Why does this writer tell you about Brian Ellis? Why does he include quotes from a doctor?

Writing for a Magazine

For this activity, you will write a magazine article. Work with one or two other students or, work on your own. Follow the steps and answer the questions below.

1. Choose a magazine you like to read. What kind of magazine is it? General interest? Special interest? Who are the main readers?

   MAGAZINE TITLE: _____

   KIND OF MAGAZINE/READERS: _____

2. Look through a recent issue. What kinds of articles are there? Which ones interest you most? Why?

   _____

3. Think of a topic that you would like to write about and that is right for the magazine. Be as specific as you can. Write your topic here.

   TOPIC: _____

4. Make an outline of your article. Where will you find the facts and details you'll need?

   _____

5. Gather your information. Revise your outline if you have extra information from your research.

6. Write a first draft of your article. Use separate paper.

7. Reread, revise and proofread your article to make it better. Check facts. Check spelling and grammar. Check punctuation.

8. Prepare a final copy. Choose a title for your article, and share your article with the class.

FOLLOW-UP

Think of another magazine you like. Suppose you were to rewrite your article for that magazine. What would you change?

Unit Test

Checking What You Have Learned

1. State whether you agree or disagree with the following statement. Explain your reasons on the lines provided.

   Advertisers can affect magazine content.

   _____

   _____

2. Two articles can handle the same topic very differently. Suppose Article 1 gives a fair, balanced view. Suppose Article 2 gives a one-sided view. To form an opinion, you should

   a. read only Article 1.

   b. read only Article 2.

   c. read both articles.

   Explain you choice.

   _____

   _____

3. A popular general interest magazine has more readers than a special interest magazine. When would it be smarter to advertise in the special interest magazine? Why?

   _____

   _____

4. Why is it important for a magazine editor to understand the target audience? Answer this essay question on a separate sheet of paper. Give examples to support your answer.

Checking How You Learned

Use the following questions to evaluate your performance in this unit.
   • What did you discover about factors that affect magazine content?
   • What did you learn about how magazines are aimed at certain readers?
   • How can analyzing what you read help you judge the content?

Advertising in the Print Media

Print ads are all around us. You see them in newspapers and magazines. They appear on posters and billboards. They even come in the mail.

More than 1,500 ad messages fly at us each day. We ignore most of them. Ads are powerful, though. Many stay in our memory.

You may not want a backpack right now. But next month you may need one. You will go to the store and look around. One brand may sound familiar. You have seen ads for it. *The backpack for kids on the move.* You never paid attention to those ads. Or did you?

Get on the Bandwagon

Advertisers want to sell products. They use many methods to persuade you to buy. One method is the **bandwagon** ad.

You may have seen bandwagons in parades. They are gaily decorated wagons in which musicians ride. People often gather around bandwagons. That is the idea behind

Figure 1

bandwagon ads. The advertiser invites you to become part of a large group. "Come on board," the ad seems to say. "Join the crowd."

Look at the ad in Figure 1. It is a bandwagon ad for sneakers. It appeared in a teen magazine. What product is the ad selling? What message is the ad sending you?

The Best and the Greatest

Another advertising method is **exaggeration**. To exaggerate means to overstate. Ads that exaggerate make products seem more or greater than they are.

Figure 2

Look at the ad in Figure 2. It appeared in a general interest magazine.

Do HEAVEN cookies truly have the *most delicious taste*? the *richest flavor*? That is a matter of opinion. But the ad makes the cookie seem like the best there is. Who is the target audience for the ad in Figure 2?

Companies often have different ads for the same product. Look at Figure 3. It is

Figure 3

another ad for HEAVEN cookies. This one appeared in a sports magazine. How does it differ from the ad in Figure 2? Why did the company create a different ad?

Figure 4

The One and Only

Some ads claim that a product is unique. A **unique claim** suggests that a product is the only one of its kind. Look at the ad in Figure 4. It appeared in a women's magazine.

The advertiser wants you to think that GLOWING does something no other shampoo can do. How does the woman in the ad help sell the product?

Questions Without Answers

Another method of advertising is the **rhetorical question**. A rhetorical question does not expect an answer. You just read the question and think, Yes. Look at the ad in Figure 5. What questions does it ask? Who is the target audience?

Political Ads

Most ads are **product ads**. They sell products. However, there are also **political ads**. Political ads "sell" candidates.

Political ads use the same methods that product ads use. Here are some examples:

Bandwagon: *Anyone who knows this city will vote for Jones.*

Exaggeration: *Jones is the best candidate who has ever run for mayor.*

Unique claim: *No one can do the job like Jones.*

Rhetorical question: *Isn't it time for a change?*

Figure 5

Answer the following questions about advertising.

1. You have read about several ad methods. Which one do you think works best? Why?

_____

_____

2. Describe an ad you have seen that uses one of the methods. What product is the ad selling? Who is the target audience? What message is the ad sending?

_____

_____

Reading Between the Lines

Newspapers and magazines are filled with words. These words are powerful. They inform us. They entertain us. They convince us of new ideas. They try to sell us products.

Critical readers read with care. They think about the meaning of words. They also think about the feelings behind words.

Critical readers ask what a writer's purpose is. They ask if the writer has told the whole story, or only one side.

In Unit 1, you learned about newspapers. You learned that there are different kinds of papers. They cover all sorts of news. You learned that some articles report events. Other articles mix fact and opinion.

In Unit 2, you learned about magazines. You learned that some magazines try to appeal to a range of readers. But most aim only at certain readers. You also learned how advertisers can affect magazine content.

Have you heard the expression, "read between the lines"? It means to see a hidden meaning or purpose. It also means to know when writers imply or suggest something.

For this project, you will create a *Read Between the Lines* booklet. Your booklet will help readers read newspapers and magazines critically. It will give tips for "reading between the lines."

STEP 1

Getting Started........................

Work in a small group to plan the contents of your booklet. Your booklet should have at least five pages. Use large sheets of paper.

You will divide each page of your booklet into two parts. One side of each page will contain articles or ads that you find. The other side will contain your tips for reading between the lines.

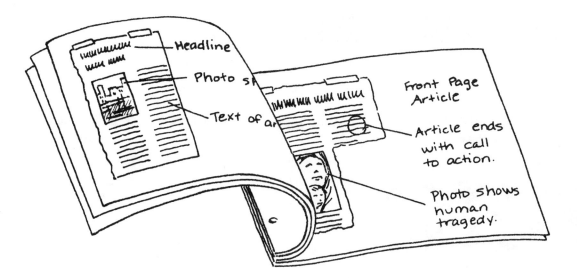

Here are some suggestions for articles or ads that you might include:
- Articles from mainstream newspapers and tabloids (You may want to include more than one article about the same event.)
- Newspaper editorials and columns
- Articles from general interest magazines
- Articles from special interest magazines
- Full-page magazine advertisements
- Eye-catching headlines and photos

Include as many articles or ads as you like. You may put more than one on a page.

Choosing Articles and Ads.......

Work as a group to choose articles and ads. Begin by looking through newspapers and magazines. Cut out or photocopy items. Set them aside. Look for items that are interesting or unusual. Discuss each item that you have set aside. Use the following checklist to guide your discussion.

READING BETWEEN THE LINES

- ❏ Does the item mislead readers in any way?
- ❏ Can readers tell the facts from the opinions?
- ❏ Does the writer say one thing but imply another?
- ❏ Is the writer trying to inform or persuade?
- ❏ How does the ad try to influence readers?

Choose the best items. Be sure to include a variety, such as:
- Hard news and soft news
- International, national, and local news
- Sports, business, and entertainment items
- Articles and ads aimed at different target audiences

Once you have made your choices, paste or tape the items on the large sheets of paper. You may want to put two related items on the same page.

Writing Tips..

Decide what tips for reading between the lines to give for each item. Use the following questions to help you.

Discuss each question with group members. Then write tips based on your answers.

FOR NEWSPAPER ARTICLES

1. Does the article imply or suggest anything?

_____

2. Does the writer give a fair account of events?

_____

3. Does the writer leave out important information?

_____

FOR MAGAZINE ARTICLES

1. Does the writer imply or suggest anything?

_____

2. What is the writer's purpose? Is there more than one purpose?

_____

3. What are the feelings behind the words?

_____

FOR EDITORIALS AND COLUMNS

1. What is the writer's purpose? Is there more than one purpose?

_____

2. What are the feelings behind the words?

_____

3. Has the writer given a balanced view of the issue?

_____

FOR ADS

1. What is the message behind the ad?

_____

2. Is the ad misleading?

_____

PHOTOS

1. What is the photo's purpose? Is there more than one purpose?

_____

2. What does the photo add to the story?

_____

STEP 4

Evaluating the Booklets................

Share your work with the class. As you look at the other groups' booklets, compare them with your own. Discuss such questions as these:

- Did the tips help you read between the lines?
- Did the items chosen serve as good examples?
- Did the tips focus on important points?
- Did the tips make you stop and think?
- What did you learn from the booklet?

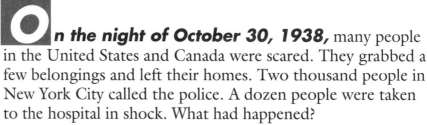

PART 2

FOCUS ON AUDIO MEDIA

ATTACK FROM MARS!

On the night of October 30, 1938, many people in the United States and Canada were scared. They grabbed a few belongings and left their homes. Two thousand people in New York City called the police. A dozen people were taken to the hospital in shock. What had happened?

These people had heard a radio show about an invasion from Mars. The show was a play that was being performed on radio. But listeners thought it was a news show. They thought the show was about a real event.

This event shows that radio can be a very powerful medium. Radio and sound recordings are **audio media.** They use sound to communicate to millions of people. Radio is a broadcast medium. It sends electronic signals through the air. The signals travel from a radio station to radio receivers. Recordings capture and store sounds on plastic disks and tape. Both radio and sound recordings developed from inventions made in the late 1800s.

Today there are more than 10,000 radio stations in the United States. Americans own about a half billion radios. They buy almost two billion compact disks (CDs) a year.

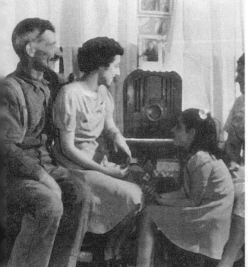

PROGRAMMING People listen to radio for two main reasons. They listen for information and they listen for entertainment. Information radio broadcasts news programs and talk shows.

Entertainment radio broadcasts music programs. There are recordings for all kinds of music. These include rock, pop, rap, country, and folk. They also include rhythm and blues, jazz, and classical.

Entertainment radio also has sports and opinion shows. The opinion shows are sometimes called "inflammation" talk shows. About 1,000 radio stations broadcast only talk shows. The rest carry music, news, and sports shows.

AUDIENCE Radio broadcasts reach millions of people every day. Different kinds of programs attract different kinds of people. Surveys show that most listeners of talk shows are politically conservative and vote Republican. Teenagers listen mostly to music radio. Only about 4 percent of Americans listen to classical music stations.

Most audiences listen to FM (frequency modulation) stations. Only about 25 percent listen to AM (amplitude modulation) stations.

FUNDING Radio broadcasting costs money. Most stations pay their costs and earn profits by broadcasting commercials. A few stations are members of National Public Radio. These stations do not have commercials. Instead, they get money from listeners and businesses.

Commercial radio stations broadcast advertisements. The ads are aimed at special audiences. The rate paid by advertisers depends on the size of the audience. It also depends on the time of day at which the ad is broadcast. This time is called the **time slot.** The rate for an ad on one "hot" talk show is $2,000 a minute.

IMPACT Radio has had a huge influence on American culture. Before television, radio helped create national heroes. These were people whose deeds were described on radio.

Radio also helped singers and other performers become "stars." Presidents gave radio talks from the White House. These talks helped inform and cheer people during hard times.

Talk shows have united people in political action. Radio broadcasts during wartime boosted the spirits of soldiers overseas.

Today, radio continues to be an important source of information and entertainment in people's lives.

CRITICAL ISSUES Radio and recordings have their share of controversy. Some people complain that talk radio promotes hatred and fear. Others complain about talk show hosts who encourage listeners to buy certain products. People complain about the broadcasting of music with lyrics they find offensive. Some radio stations have banned certain kinds of music. In return, performers complain that their music is being censored.

In Part 2, we will explore some of the issues concerning radio and recordings.

UNIT 1   Information Talk Radio

If you have ever "surfed" the AM stations on your radio, you have probably come across information talk shows. These are shows in which an expert gives information and answers questions from callers. The expert is usually the host of the show. The host runs the show, answers callers' questions, and sometimes even presents advertisements for a sponsor's product or service. The host may be an expert on a subject such as gardening, money matters, legal matters, health care, personal problems, or pet care. Or the host may interview experts on a subject. Callers' questions are usually "screened" for relevance to the topic before they are allowed on the air.

In the following play, two teenagers have different views about an information talk show. Read the play aloud with other members of your class.

Who's Talking
A Play in One Act and One Scene

CAST: Michelle (high school student)
           Raul (Michelle's older brother)
           Dr. Lynn Marcus (talk show host)
           Maria (caller)

Setting
(*The kitchen of Michelle's home. Michelle is sitting at the table with her notebook and school books, half studying, but also listening to the radio. The radio is tuned to a talk show called "Ask Dr. Lynn." As Michelle listens, we hear the talk show in progress.*)

DR. LYNN: Good afternoon! I'm Dr. Lynn Marcus. Give me a call at 1-800-555-LYNN. Today I'd like to focus on feelings involved with friendships. What is a friend anyway? How do you express your friendship? Friendships have ups and downs, too. Learning to be a good friend is one of life's most valuable lessons. Give me a call at 1-800-555-LYNN—that's 1-800-555- 5966. I see we have a call from Maria in Rochester. Hello, Maria! How can I help you?

MARIA: Hi, Dr. Lynn. This is, like, sort of an embarrassing question.

DR. LYNN: Uh huh, I'm listening....

MARIA: Well, one of my girlfriends is like, really, really smart. Like she helps me with my homework and stuff, and she's a nice person and all that, but there's something about her that sort of bothers me.

(*At this point, Michelle's older brother Raul enters the kitchen and goes to the refrigerator to get something to eat.*)

RAUL: Hi, Michelle. Whatcha listening to?

MICHELLE: Shhh! It's Dr. Lynn and I want to hear this girl's question.

(*Michelle turns up the radio and moves closer to it.*)

MARIA:....well, I mean it's her breath. When she talks to me, I sort of have to take a breath myself and hold it because it smells—I mean her breath.

DR. LYNN: And you're afraid to tell her about her breath....

RAUL: You're listening to that crap? Don't you know those talk show people are just nuts?

MICHELLE: Raul, you don't know anything about it. Dr. Lynn is on WBRC every afternoon, and she gives advice to teenagers.

RAUL: (*smirking*) I could give you advice....What kind of doctor is she? An animal doctor?

MICHELLE: (*clenching her jaw*) Very funny. She's a psychologist.

RAUL: How do you know?

On talk shows, listeners call in their questions. This makes the shows spontaneous and relevant to everyday people.

The caller can ask uncomfortable questions because she is calling anonymously.

Dr. Lynn has not said much about her credentials—her title, training, and experience. What would you need to know in order to believe that she's a real psychologist?

MICHELLE: Well...she says she is.

(*Radio voice up*)

DR. LYNN: You probably have put yourself in her place. And you imagine what might happen if someone told you you had bad breath.

MARIA: Right.

DR. LYNN: But you're not just anyone. You're her—what's her name?

MARIA: Carmel.

DR. LYNN: Carmel—you're her best friend. Wouldn't you rather be told something a little embarrassing by your best friend than by a stranger?

MARIA: I'm not sure. I'd be pretty embarrassed. I mean it would just kill me.

> Do you think Dr. Lynn has shown that she knows what she's talking about? What else might she do or say to show her credibility?

DR. LYNN: You might feel like you were dying, but you wouldn't be, really. I think you'd live through it. And, you know, there are ways you could tell Carmel without being rude. For example, you might buy some breath mints. Take one yourself and ask her if she'd like one. Tell her they're really good for covering up bad breath and that you think she might like to try one....

(*Michelle's voice interrupts*)

MICHELLE: You see...She's really nice, and she's helpful. People call in with all kind of questions and she helps them.

RAUL: Yeah, sure. What's she selling?

MICHELLE: (*annoyed*) What?

> Many talk shows are sponsored by companies that pay to have their advertisements read on the show.

RAUL: These talk show hosts are always trying to get you to buy something. I heard about this guy on a talk show who got people to buy shares of stock in companies that didn't even exist. Then the guy took the money—millions of dollars—and left the country!

MICHELLE: Well, Dr. Lynn's not like that. I don't think she's ripping anybody off.

(*Radio voice up. Dr. Lynn's voice.*)

DR. LYNN: ...and speaking of choices, I'd like to tell you about *Today's Teens* magazine, the magazine created with you in mind. It's the magazine I hope you'll choose to read. Every month you'll find articles on health, fashions, celebrities, dating, study tips, and much, much more. To subscribe and get your free *Today's Teens* T-shirt, call 1-800-555-TEEN, that's 1-800-555-TEEN. I recommend *Today's Teens* for teens who want to be informed.

RAUL: You see! She's selling some stupid magazine! That's all she wants you to do is buy something.

MICHELLE: Raul! You haven't even read the magazine, so don't call it stupid.

RAUL: Have *you* read it? I hope you didn't buy a subscription. Mom will have a fit. That's all we need is one more magazine.

MICHELLE: Well, it can't be that bad if Dr. Lynn recommends it. After all, she's very helpful.

RAUL: So maybe you should call in and ask her to send you a free copy.

MICHELLE: I'm going to call in and ask her about a dorky brother who doesn't think she's for real.

Notice how Dr. Lynn smoothly begins talking about the magazine. She is making a commercial announcement. Do you think the sponsor is pleased to have her reading the commercial? Why?

◀ The sponsor of Dr. Lynn's show is a magazine called *Today's Teens*. The magazine has paid the station and Dr. Lynn to present its advertisement. What other companies might be interested in advertising on Dr. Lynn's show? Why?

◀ Some listeners may buy a product because they believe the talk show host is a good authority. how could listeners find out more about a product before they buy it?

Lesson 1
Are You Really Listening?

You use your ears a lot, but do you analyze what you hear? Critical listening is a skill. It is the ability to analyze what you are listening to. It takes time and practice. Critical listening helps you form opinions about what you hear. When you listen critically, you can decide if the information you hear is true or not true, useful or not useful. Critical listening helps you get the information you really want.

When you listen to information radio, think critically about what you're hearing. While you're tuned in, ask yourself questions such as these:

- Does the expert's information or advice seem believable?
- Who might be interested in listening to the program?
- Does the expert have a particular viewpoint? What is it?
- Is there another way of looking at the topic? What is it?

Here is an excerpt from another talk show. The expert is 17-year-old Jeffrey Chung. Jeffrey has become successful at making money on the stock market.

JEFFREY: Don't be afraid of stocks! You can learn about them as I did, and I started when I was eight years old. How did I start? I was curious. I'd heard news stories about the stock market. I'd heard about prices going up and down, people making lots of money and people losing money. I decided to find out everything I could about stocks. I spent weeks reading information in the library. I took notes. I asked questions. I even called in to a couple of information talk shows. Then, when I felt I had enough information, I bought my first shares of stock in a company. I was too young to buy them myself, so my parents bought them for me.... I'm going to take a call now from Carolyn in Topeka. Hello, Carolyn. What's your question?

CAROLYN: Hi, Jeffrey. I'd like to know how to tell which stocks to buy.

JEFFREY: My advice, Carolyn, is to stay away from big companies and big stocks. They're expensive, to start with. But secondly, the values can go up and down suddenly. People who own these stocks sometimes get nervous. When they hear bad news, they tend to sell. That drives down the value of the stock. A third reason is that there are a lot of smart people investing in big stocks. They know these stocks well. It's hard to outsmart them.

What you want to do is look for small companies. Look for companies with unusual services or products. Then, before you invest, study, study, study. Find out as much as you can about the company. Read its annual report. Read what the business magazines say about it. Look for a company that has grown by at least 20 percent a year for a few years. That growth lets you know the company is probably a good bet.

Let me give you an example. A few years ago, I invested in a company that owns several animal hospitals. The hospitals are located around the country. The company is backed by a big pet food maker. Pets are popular. They get sick and need care, just like people. Pet owners spend lots of money to take care of them. The company has done well so far. I expect it to continue.

I have another caller now. Hello, I'm Jeffrey. What's your question?....

Talk radio stations schedule certain programs at certain times of the day. They do this to attract certain kinds of listeners. A mid-day show may be aimed at people who are likely to be at home and not at an office. At what time of day do you think Jeffrey's show would be scheduled? Why?

Notice how Jeffrey makes listeners aware of his credentials. Also notice how Jeffrey sets the tone for the program. How does he try to keep listeners tuned-in and interested?

When you **analyze** something, you think about it carefully, part by part. You ask yourself questions as you think about each part: What is this about? What supporting evidence is there? Is the evidence valid? What is the purpose? Your questions help you understand each part. By understanding each part, you also have a better understanding of the whole thing.

To evaluate means to make a judgment about something. Is it good? Why is it good? How well does it do what it is supposed to do? Questions like these help you when you are evaluating something.

What do you think of Jeffrey's advice? Answer the following questions about his advice.

1. What is Jeffrey's viewpoint regarding stocks?

   _____

   _____

   _____

2. What is another viewpoint that a different expert on stocks might have?

   _____

   _____

   _____

3. What is Jeffrey's main point about buying stocks?

   _____

   _____

   _____

4. What evidence shows that Jeffrey is an expert on stocks?

   _____

   _____

   _____

5. Which of Jeffrey's ideas makes the most sense to you? What would you want Jeffrey to explain further?

   _____

   _____

   _____

6. What kinds of companies do you think would want to advertise on Jeffrey's show?

   _____

   _____

   _____

Lesson 2
The Sponsor Strategy

MICHAEL JORDAN

Some talk radio hosts are experts about gardening, health, cars, or other subjects. These hosts have special knowledge and experience. The sponsors of a show are happy to have their products endorsed by experts. A host may really believe the product is good. But the host is also paid by the sponsor to endorse the product. Should you then believe *everything* the host tells you about a product? How do you evaluate a host's credibility?

In this excerpt from an information radio broadcast, can you tell where the expert advice ends and the sales pitch begins?

DIANE: Welcome to the Diane Connors Show! I'm Diane Connors, your host and used car expert. You know, many people are amazed to learn that Americans buy more than 18 million used cars a year. But it's true. Used cars are big business. And they're big business because they're a good buy. Let's say you drive 10,000 miles a year. Let's say you buy a new car for $15,000. If you drive that car till it drops, you'll have spent about 38¢ a mile. Now suppose you bought a four-year-old used car for $7000. Suppose you drove that car until it died. You'd have spent about 26¢ a mile. Now you tell me, which is the better deal? 1-800-555-CARS, that's 1-800-555-2277. Let's take our first call from Jeremy in Scottsdale. Hello, Jeremy.

JEREMY: Hi, Diane. I'd like to buy a used car, but I'm not sure what to look for. I mean, how do I keep from buying a lemon?

MEDIA WISE

Pay close attention to Diane's example. Does she say how long it would take for your car to "drop"? How could you figure out how long she thinks that will be? Is it certain that the car would be "dead" after that length of time? Why do you think Diane uses this example?

45

DIANE: Good question, Jeremy. There are several basic things to look for inside the car, outside the car, and on the road. Let's take inside first. Is the car clean? Look at the seats and the floor. Are they clean and smooth? Look at the dashboard and control panel. Is it in good condition? Are the inside door handles in good shape? Do the windows work? Get in and sit in the driver's seat. Look around inside the car. Turn on the ignition but don't start the car. Do the controls and meters work? You know, my friends down at Columbia Sales like to tell the story about a man who came in looking for a used car. They showed him a model and he asked if it had an alarm clock. Well, Dave and José, two first-rate car dealers down at Columbia, were confused. They asked why he wanted an alarm clock in a car. The guy said, "Oh, I don't want to drive the car. I just want to sleep in it!" Well, whatever your automobile needs, you'll find a solution at Columbia Sales at the corner of Park and Freemont Avenues. Call 555-7000 and ask to see Dave or José. Tell them you heard about Columbia on the Diane Connors Show. Time for another call at 1-800-555-CARS. Hello, Juanita in Seattle. What's your question on the Diane Connors show?

How would you evaluate Diane Connors as a source of information? To reach your conclusion, respond to each question.

1. What evidence is there that Diane Connors is really an expert on used cars? Cite specific examples.

_____

_____

2. Does Diane stick to the facts in her response to the caller? Explain.

_____

_____

Now answer these questions about Diane's program and its audience.

3. Why would an audience listen to Diane's show?

_____

_____

4. Why would Columbia Sales want to sponsor Diane's show?

_____

_____

5. Why do you suppose Diane presented the advertisement for Columbia Sales herself?

_____

_____

6. Do you think Diane loses credibility by presenting the ad herself? Explain.

_____

_____

7. Do you think that by presenting the ad herself that Diane is being fair to her audience? Explain.

_____

_____

8. What could listeners do to become aware of a host's hidden agenda?

_____

_____

DISCUSSION

• •

How would you rate Diane as an expert and talk show host? Use a scale of 1 to 5, with 5 being the highest or most trustworthy. Use the chart below. Rate Diane in each category. Discuss your reasons. Then discuss whether talk show hosts should read commercials for products on their show.

The Diane Connors Show					
	Lowest				Highest
Knows Facts	1	2	3	4	5
Gives Good Advice	1	2	3	4	5
Is Not Biased or Partial	1	2	3	4	5

THE LANGUAGE OF THINKING

A **hidden agenda** is a kind of sneak attack. When Diane begins talking about Columbia Sales, she has a hidden agenda. She wants listeners to buy a car from Columbia Sales, but she does not start by saying that. Instead, she slyly changes topics—from advising Jeremy to talking about her "friends" at Columbia Sales. She tells a silly joke to charm listeners, then she gives the sales pitch. Diane is **biased** in relation to Columbia Sales. To be biased means to be unfairly for or against something or someone.

Credibility means how believable something is. You can evaluate the credibility of sources of information by asking questions. Does the information make sense? Is the information accurate? Is the information from a good or reliable source? Are the speaker's opinions fair and balanced? Do other sources agree with this one? Why might the speaker give this information?

Your answers to these questions can help you judge the credibility of sources.

Lesson 3
Station Surfing

blah, information, commercial, commercial, blah, blah, information, information, blah, commercial. blah, information, commercial, commercial, blah, information, information, blah, commercial, information, blah, information, blah.

 You now know something about information radio. What are the popular information programs in your town or city? Who are the experts? Listen to a couple of local information talk shows. Compare two shows.
- Listen to each show for at least thirty minutes.
- Complete the chart.
- Discuss your chart with your classmates.

	PROGRAM A	PROGRAM B
NAME		
HOST		
TOPIC		

	PROGRAM A	PROGRAM B
TIME SLOT	_____	_____
	_____	_____
AUDIENCE (age, interests)	_____	_____
	_____	_____
FORMAT (host does all the talking or host interviews experts)	_____	_____
	_____	_____
HOST'S CREDIBILITY	_____	_____
	_____	_____
PRODUCTS ADVERTISED	_____	_____
	_____	_____
HOW ADVERTISEMENTS ARE PRESENTED (by host or prerecorded)	_____	_____
	_____	_____

Your Conclusion

Which program was better? Why?

_____

_____

_____

_____

_____

_____

_____

_____

All the News?

Two of the ways you can get news are from the radio and from the newspaper. Each medium presents the news in a different way. In this activity, you will compare radio news and print news.

Work with a group of your classmates. Follow these steps:

- Listen to a local all-news radio broadcast for at least thirty minutes.

- Get a copy of the local newspaper for the same day that you listen to the radio news. Spend fifteen minutes reading through the paper.

- Compare the news broadcast and the newspaper. Answer these questions and discuss your responses.

    Which one gives more information?

    How is the information different in each one?

    Are stories less biased in one than in the other? In which one?

    Which one is easier to use? Why?

    Which one has a greater impact on you? Why?

    What role do advertisements play in each medium?

    In which medium are the ads more effective? Why?

    Who are the audiences for the two different media?

- On a separate sheet of paper, write your conclusions about the way each medium presents news.

Unit Test

Checking What You Have Learned

1. Information radio is different from other kinds of radio because it

   a. does not have as many commercials

   b. has experts who give advice

   c. has fewer listeners

   d. does not screen callers' questions.

   Explain your answer.

   _____

2. Put an *X* next to the statement that is true. Explain your choice on the lines provided.

   ❑ Critical listening helps you analyze what you hear.

   ❑ A program's time slot has very little to do with its audience.

   _____

   _____

3. Why do you think an expert would personally make a commercial announcement for a company? Use examples and details to support your answer.

   _____

4. Why is it important to evaluate both the information and the advertisements presented by an information radio host? Answer this essay question on a separate sheet of paper. Support your answer with examples and details.

Checking How You Learned

Use the following questions to help you evaluate your performance in this unit.
- How did you use listening skills to analyze what the speaker was saying?
- In listening to an information radio host, how can you tell if the host is a good source of information?
- What similarities and differences did you recognize between programs? How can you improve your ability to listen critically?

You may have listened to a kind of talk radio that seems different from information radio. It does not give advice or information. It stirs up listeners and lets them express their opinions about a topic. Some people have called this type of radio "inflammation" radio. When something is inflamed, it is burning out of control. On this kind of radio show, you may hear people who sound "out of control." Some hosts and callers shout, make political attacks, and call people ugly names. Inflammation radio can be strong stuff. When you tune in, you will need to fasten your safety belt. In the following example, talk show host Jerry Knight has some strong feelings about jails and people in jails.

▶ Jerry Knight's attitude is tough on crime. Do you think his argument would persuade anyone who had a different point of view. Why or why not?

JERRY KNIGHT: As I said, folks, it's time to toughen up the jails. Nowadays nobody's afraid to go to jail. Why? Because jails are cushy. They're comfortable. You get arrested, you can live better in jail than you can outside. You take some of these homeless bums, they're going around—they don't even have to mug anybody. They just have to be someplace where they shouldn't be. They make a nuisance of themselves. Then the cops arrest them, and *whammo!* they're home free. They've got a roof over their head, three meals a day, TV, books to read. This is *punishment*? Come on! No wonder we've got a crime wave!

Did you read the story about the one-legged guy who was thrown in jail? He made a fuss because they took away his crutches! The nerve! And then you have these bleeding hearts who say, "Oh the poor guy; he's got only one leg. It's *not fair!*" Hey, folks, this guy's a *criminal!* I say *take away the crutches*. We can't have a crutch-waving madman in our jail. A crutch is a weapon. We've got to protect our police and jail wardens. And suppose this low-life bum gets into a fight with another prisoner. Suppose the other guy hits old peg-leg hip-hop with his own crutch. Then what? One-leg could turn around and sue the state for millions of dollars. Now that would be a fine story for your soft-on-crime woosies. I can see the headlines now: GOES TO JAIL AND BECOMES A MILLIONAIRE!

Folks, I think it's time for *no frills jail!* Bread and water, that's all they should feed them. Forget TVs, radios, newspapers, magazines, books. I don't want MY tax dollars paying to *educate* some lousy *crime jerk*. Let 'em sit and count their toes, I say, even if they only have five of them. And *no presents or gifts* from family and friends. What is this? You go to jail and people act like it's your birthday or something. No way! The sleep-away camp is over, folks. I say, let's make our jails so tough, somebody'll think twice before committing a crime.

What do you have to say about this? The lines are open. 1-800-555-3500. I'm Jerry Knight, the Knight-watcher, here on WKLU, "Stimulating Talk."

◀ Notice the way Jerry Knight expresses judgments, such as "The nerve!" and "Now that would be a fine story." Notice how he uses name calling—words like "bum" and "bleeding hearts." Notice how he turns words like "comfortable," and "punishment" into loaded words that have strong emotional meaning. How might someone with a different point of view respond to his ideas?

◀ A biased viewpoint leans to only one side of an argument. It is not balanced. What evidence of bias do you see in Jerry Knight's comments? Why might a show like Jerry's be popular?

You might agree or disagree with a talk show host. Either way, you have to admit that the host is a powerful person. For a half hour, hour, or more, the host is boss of the air waves. Millions of listeners hear the host's viewpoint and comments. Sometimes the format of the show lets listeners call in to express their ideas.

Some hosts welcome only those callers whose ideas agree with theirs. A host may cut off a caller who expresses an opposing idea. A host may listen to a caller with an opposing opinion but then "trash" the person for daring to disagree. To tell if a host is being objective or fair, listen for these behaviors:

- Does the host consider another point of view about a topic?
- Does the host allow callers who disagree to have their say?
- Does the host avoid techniques such as name calling, loaded words, exaggeration, and expressing judgments?

You can tell a lot about a host from the way he or she talks to callers. Read the following excerpt from the Phyllis Cole program. What do you notice about the way the host treats two different callers?

PHYLLIS: We're talking about sports heroes today on the Phyllis Cole show. Call in and let me hear your opinion—at 1-800-555-2778. Have you noticed that there are fewer and fewer sports stars who DESERVE our respect? What happened to the good old days when sports stars were *respectable people?* They were models of good behavior—clean, decent, hard-working, courageous. What do we have today? A bunch of pill popping, drug dealing, alcoholic professional bad boys. Are these good models for our children? Let's hear from Damond in Biloxi.

DAMOND: Hi, Phyllis. I'd like to disagree with you. I don't think sports stars are any different today than they were twenty or thirty or even fifty years ago....

PHYLLIS: *Ex-cuse* me, Damond. What planet have you been on lately? Clearly, not planet Earth. Call back after you re-enter. [*Click*] Let's hear from Claudia in Fargo.

CLAUDIA: Hi, Phyllis. I absolutely agree with you. My teenage son just worships some of these sports jerks. And I try to tell him, honey, these guys are not worth your time.

PHYLLIS: Good for you, Claudia.

CLAUDIA: I mean they make all this money—millions of dollars— and then they behave like punks! And nobody cares if they've broken the law. It's like they're above the law somehow.

PHYLLIS: Absolutely, Claudia! If you or I acted like that, we'd be run out of town. But these guys are welcomed back with open arms. They're given new contracts—for more millions. Thanks for your call, Claudia. I could use more callers like you!

What did you notice about the way Phyllis treated her two callers?

1. Was Phyllis fair to Damond? How could you tell?

_____

_____

2. What did Phyllis imply about Damond?

_____

_____

Notice Phyllis's use of loaded words such as "clean" and "decent." Notice her name calling. Another technique of propaganda is **hasty generalization.** Phyllis lumps all professional sports players into one group—"a bunch of...." Is this fair? Are all players alike?

3. Do you think Damond might have been able to make a good argument against Phyllis? Why or why not?

_____

_____

4. In what ways was Phyllis Cole not objective?

_____

_____

5. What clues indicate that Phyllis has a different attitude toward Claudia?

_____

_____

6. Would you be willing to call into Phyllis's show and express your opinion? Why or why not?

_____

_____

Lesson 2
Hearing Both Sides

You hear plenty of opinions on talk radio. How do you decide which opinions to agree with? How can you form your own opinion on a topic? One way to decide is to evaluate an argument you hear. Here are some tips:

- Pick out the speaker's main point.
- Notice how the speaker supports the main point. Are the supporting facts, examples, and ideas convincing? Do they make sense?
- Be aware of any propaganda techniques the speaker may use. As you saw in Lesson 1, these include name calling, biased opinions, lies, exaggeration, loaded words, and hasty generalizations.
- Be aware of your own bias. You may find that you agree with someone because you *already* believe as they do, even though the person's argument is not strong. Try to set aside your own opinion until you evaluate both arguments.

Read the following excerpt from the Ray Noble Show. Pay close attention to the way the host and caller present their arguments.

Hasty generalizations often use words such as "every," "all," "none," "never," and "always." Another propaganda technique is the **misleading statement.** A misleading statement suggests that something is true that is not really true. Ray Noble suggests that the streets would be safe if teenagers were locked up. Why might that not be true?

Yolanda avoids generalizing by using the word "most." She does not say "all" or "every." Words like "most," "some" and "few" are called **qualifiers.**

RAY NOBLE: I've said it before. I'll say it again. Every town and city in this country should have a teen curfew. Teenagers should not be allowed to wander the streets at all hours of the night. These punks are just looking for trouble. I say lock 'em up and make the streets safe. I have a call from Yolanda in Mount Vernon. Hi Yolanda.

YOLANDA: Hi, Mr. Noble. I'm a teenager, and I think curfews are wrong. This is a free country. We're teenagers, but we're also *people*. We have rights just like anybody else. A curfew takes away some of those rights. I think our parents should be allowed to decide if we can go out at night. Most parents would probably keep their kids indoors after dark, anyway.

RAY NOBLE: What do you know about parents? *I'm* a parent, and I see other parents who don't care. Where were the parents of that fourteen-year-old kid who was killed on the streets of Newark at 12:40 in the morning?

YOLANDA: Those kids are exceptions. Most kids are law-abiding. And besides, Mr. Noble, the police have better things to do than look after teenagers on the streets. A lot of cities already have curfews, the curfews are not enforced because the police don't have time to enforce them.

RAY NOBLE: Well, I don't think there's anything more important than cutting down on teenage crime and teenage deaths. Teenage crime is sweeping the nation.

YOLANDA: What about all the crimes that *adults* commit?

Use the chart to write each speaker's main points.

RAY NOBLE	YOLANDA
_____	_____
_____	_____
_____	_____
_____	_____
_____	_____
_____	_____
_____	_____
_____	_____
_____	_____

1. How well does Ray Noble support his main points? Explain your opinion.

_____

_____

_____

2. How well does Yolanda support her main points? Explain your opinion.

_____

_____

_____

3. How does listening to Ray Noble and Yolanda help you make up your own mind about the topic?

_____

_____

_____

4. What more could you do in order to make up your own mind about the topic?

_____

_____

_____

5. Do you think an "inflammation" talk show is a good place to hear both sides of an issue? Explain your answer.

_____

_____

_____

Lesson 3
Forming Your Own Opinion

Should you believe everything you hear on talk radio? How can you tell what's worthwhile and what's not? One solution is to develop **criteria** or standards. These can help you make choices about ideas and information you hear.

Suppose you were going to buy a sweater. You would use criteria or standards to choose your sweater. Your first criterion would be the purpose of the sweater. Will you wear it for special occasions, or is it for everyday wear? Your purpose helps you decide on other criteria. These might be a certain color, a certain kind of fabric, a certain style, a nice feel when you touch it. You don't want any flaws in it. You use these criteria to evaluate the sweaters you see. Some sweaters fit your criteria. Others do not.

You can use the same method in evaluating what you hear on a talk radio show. The following chart lists some criteria you can use. Fill out the chart.

Criteria are rules, standards, or tests used to make a judgment or decision. Your criteria for something may be different from someone else's. The word **criteria** is plural. The singular is **criterion**.

SHOW: _____

HOST: _____

YOUR PURPOSE FOR LISTENING: ❏ Entertainment
    (*check one*)   ❏ Ideas
                               ❏ Information

CRITERIA	EVALUATION
Host's tone of voice	
Host's use of slang words or name calling	
Fairness of host's ideas	
Host's fairness to callers or to guests on the program	
Accuracy of host's information	

Add other criteria of your own. Then use the chart to evaluate an "inflammation" talk show. Listen to a show for at least thirty minutes. In the evaluation column, write your opinion of what you hear. You might evaluate each criterion as "good," "average," or "poor." You might use a number system, such as 1-5, with 1 being "poor" and 5 "excellent." Then write a paragraph or two summarizing your evaluation of the program. Discuss the program and your evaluation with your classmates.

Debating Radio

There are about 10,000 radio stations in the United States. Just over 1,000 of these are talk radio stations. One of the most popular shows is broadcast on 660 stations and has 20 million listeners. From these facts, you can see that talk radio is an important part of American life.

Yet some people are alarmed at what they hear on talk radio. They say talk radio brings out the worst in hosts, listeners, and callers. They hear expressions of hatred, fear, and anger. They worry about the use of talk radio for political purposes. Still other people are great fans of talk radio. They listen faithfully. Only a small percent of listeners call into the shows. Yet those callers are glad to have a chance to express their opinions. They want their opinions heard.

DEBATE

Now that you know something about "inflammation" radio, express your ideas about it. In a small group, debate the pros and cons of this kind of radio. You may want to spend time listening to a few more programs before you start your debate. Then choose one of these questions to debate, or make up a debate question of your own.

- Is talk radio good for people?
- Are talk radio hosts biased?
- Does talk radio promote hatred and fear?
- Should there be rules to limit some of the things that talk show hosts can say on the air?

RULES OF DEBATE

- Set a time limit for the debate.
- Give each debater a chance to present his or her point of view.
- Allow time for other debaters to comment on the different points of view.
- Evaluate and discuss the results of the debate.

Unit Test

Checking What You Have Learned

1. Mark the best answer with an *X*. Explain your reasons on the lines provided.

"Inflammation" radio is different from other talk radio programs because it

❏ has hosts and listeners who call in.

❏ sticks strictly to facts and information.

❏ expresses strong opinions about topics.

_____

_____

2. Put an *X* next to the statements that are true. Explain your choices.

❏ A biased host listens to all points of view.

❏ A biased host does not welcome opposing points of view.

❏ To persuade an audience, a host may use propaganda methods.

❏ Propaganda is the use of objective methods of persuasion.

_____

_____

_____

3. How can criteria help you listen to an "inflammation" radio program? Answer this essay question on a separate sheet of paper. Give examples to support your answer.

Checking How You Learned

Use the following questions to evaluate your performance in this unit.
- What methods did you learn for evaluating an "inflammation" talk show host?
- Were you able to identify criteria of your own to use in listening to a radio program? If not, what can you do to learn how to form criteria?
- How can developing and using criteria help you in other parts of your life?

63

Advertising on Radio

Radio was the first medium to have **commercials.** A commercial is an advertisement that is broadcast. On radio, advertisements can be shaped to appeal to listeners. Radio ads can use voices, dialogue, sound effects, and music. Here is a sample from a script for a radio advertisement.

(*"Home" type sounds up. Sound of dishes, knives, and forks being placed on table*)

MOTHER: Dinner's ready! Jake, Are you going to wash that paint off your hands before you eat?

JAKE: I tried, Mom, but you know that hand soap you bought is not for tough jobs. I'll wait till later when I have time to really scrub.

ANNOUNCER: Does this sound like your house? Is your hand soap not tough enough for tough jobs? Now's the time to switch to Deep Clean, the soap that's hard on dirt but gentle on your hands.

(*sound of water running in sink*)

JAKE: Hey, Mom, you know this new soap really cleans fast. Good smell, too.

The first radio ads were not much more than print ads read by an announcer. But soon, advertisers began using more sophisticated ad techniques. You've already seen how sponsors and hosts may have a **hidden agenda.** Remember Diane Connors

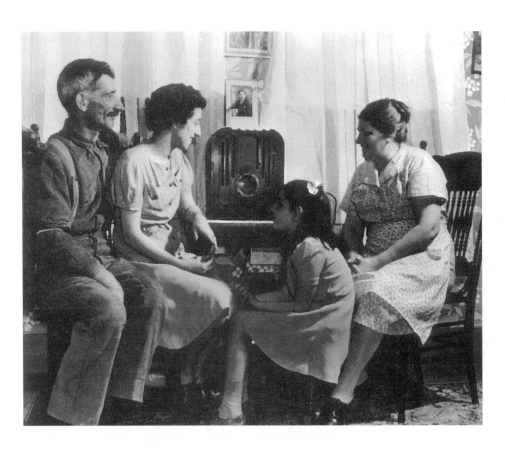

and her "friends" at Columbia Sales? Two other advertising techniques are the **vague** claim and the **endorsement** or **testimonial.** In the vague claim, something positive but not very clear is said about the product. In the exerpt on page 64, notice the claim, "...the soap that's hard on dirt but gentle on your hands." How can listeners know this soap is effective against all kinds of dirt? How can they know it's "gentle" to people's hands? The sponsors have probably not done scientific tests to find out. Even if it were true, the claim does not tell you whether the soap is any better than other soaps like it.

In the endorsement or testimonial, a celebrity encourages listeners to try a product. The person may be a celebrity or someone playing a part. The commercial uses the person's fame, title, or acting ability to persuade listeners that the product is good. Advertisers pay celebrities to endorse their products. They also pay actors to read testimonial ads. In the illustration on page 64, you can see someone who is listening to a celebrity endorsement.

As in all advertising, sponsors of radio shows want to reach the widest audience. To do so, they choose programs that have a popular time slot. They may also choose shows that have a special topic. The topic must have a clear "tie in" or close relationship, to the sponsor's product. A company that makes plant food, for example, would be likely to advertise on a gardening talk show.

Spend fifteen minutes listening to radio commercials. Then answer the questions about radio commercials. Work with a group of your classmates to do the activity.

1. Describe a vague claim you have heard in a commercial. What makes the claim vague?

   _____

2. Describe a celebrity radio commercial. What product is the commercial advertising? Who was the celebrity? What program was the commercial sponsoring?

   _____

ACTIVITY: On a separate sheet of paper, write a script for a radio commercial. Use some of the advertising techniques you have learned about in this section.

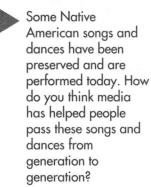

Some Native American songs and dances have been preserved and are performed today. How do you think media has helped people pass these songs and dances from generation to generation?

It is everywhere, any time of day. People wake up to it and go to sleep by it. We study with it. We work to it. We worship with it, dance to it, and relax to it. We argue over it and fight for it. We spend lots of money on it. We can not imagine life without it. Take a close look at almost any human event. You will find music somewhere close by. In fact, there probably has not been much human life on this planet without music.

Suppose you could take a musical time machine back into American history. You would find that music has played a role in many important events.

Long before Europeans came to North America, songs and dances were an important part of Native American culture. The first Americans worshipped and celebrated with songs and dances.

Pilgrims sang hymns to express their thanks for arriving in a new land. The song "Yankee Doodle" helped General Washington's soldiers defeat the British. Enslaved Africans sang songs that helped them survive and escape slavery.

During the Civil War, military bands played tunes such as "Dixie," "The Battle Hymn of the Republic," and "When Johnny Comes Marching Home."

Moving your time machine forward a bit, you will see symphony orchestras forming about 1900. These American groups were modeled after European orchestras. American orchestras first appeared in Boston, Chicago, Philadelphia, New York, and Minneapolis. About the same time, musical theater grew from minstrel shows into vaudeville and burlesque. In minstrel shows, men sang, danced, and played musical instruments. The shows also included comedy routines. Both African American and white men performed as minstrels. Vaudeville and burlesque were also entertainment shows. They were made up of several short acts performed by different people. Songs from these shows became part of America's popular music around the turn of the century.

As African Americans moved from rural areas to cities, they brought new forms of music with them. The first was ragtime, a jumpy style of piano playing. Another was the blues—slow, sometimes sad songs. These two kinds of music led to a third kind of music called jazz.

Push your time machine forward to 1920–1945. You will see that music helped Americans through the Great Depression. Two of the most popular songs were "Stormy Weather," and "Brother Can You Spare a Dime?" The titles give you a hint of the difficult times Americans faced.

Jazz bands, popular singers, and Broadway musicals helped Americans fight and celebrate victory in two World Wars. A new invention—radio—sent music into millions of homes.

As you enter the 1950s, hold on tight. The music scene began to shake, rattle, and roll with a new sound: rock 'n' roll. This music had its roots in African Americans' rhythm and blues. Early forms of rock 'n' roll were performed by white as well as black performers. Some of the stars have become legendary. You can still hear recordings by Elvis Presley, Chuck Berry, and Ruth Brown on many radio stations today.

Soon after rock 'n' roll burst on the scene, other music forms began to carve their own place in American music. These included country and western music and rock music. These also included "pure" rhythm and blues, gospel, folk, and "pop" or popular music. Thanks to new ways of making records and to the rise of FM stations, Americans had more music than they could ever listen to.

The first radio broadcasts in America included symphonic music and songs from American musical theater. This music was performed live in radio studios.

Jazz was introduced to Europe in the 1920s by recordings. In America, recordings were very popular. Twenty-five million records were sold in 1917. When radio became popular in the late 1920s, record producers were alarmed. They thought people would stop buying records. The sound was better on radios than on records. For awhile, radio ruled. Then in the late 1940s the long-playing record was invented. Recordings and radio have been partners ever since.

As your time machine hovers over the 1960s and 1970s, you will see the Civil Rights Movement. You will see protests against the Vietnam War. Also, you will hear music in each of these events. Civil Rights marchers sang spirituals, hymns, and folk songs. So did protesters against the Vietnam War. Songs such as "We Shall Overcome," "Where Have All the Flowers Gone?," and "Give Peace a Chance" helped people express their beliefs about America's social and political conditions. Music helped these people attempt to achieve their goals.

In another part of the 1970s, the beat goes on. It is disco music. The sound is both hard and mellow. Then in the 1980s, hip hop and salsa are hot. Then comes rap. Millions of recordings are spinning. The music is everywhere. It's on radio and in the movies. It's on stage, on TV, on CDs and cassettes, and in concerts. America's musical mix grows wider and wider.

As you cruise back to the present, what do you notice about the music you hear? What role does it play in the events of this time?

Lesson 1
Categories of Music Stations

When you turn on the radio, what kind of station do you listen to? As you know, there are several kinds of stations to choose from. Most stations have a special format. One station may play mostly jazz, for example. Another station plays classic rock. Another plays top 40 recordings. There are also formats such as "Lite," "Cool," and "Oldies." These formats may include different categories of music. An oldie, for example, may be a rock 'n' roll, pop, country, or rhythm and blues song.

Each station has a target audience. These are the people station owners want to listen to their station. Audiences are identified by demographics. These are facts such as age, place of residence, and income. One station may have a target audience that is 18 to 30 years old. That audience may also live in a rural area and have an income of $5,000 to $25,000 a year. Another station may have a target audience of 12- to 24-year-olds who live in an urban area. That audience might have an income of $0 to $30,000 a year.

To capture and keep an audience, radio stations have several strategies. They play five minutes of commercials and then ten or fifteen minutes of music, nonstop. They may mix music in a certain way—for example always beginning the hour with an up-tempo song.

Stations may provide features such as contests, hourly news, and weather reports. They may also have call-in request hours and traffic reports.

Categories help you organize information. You group items that are similar into one category. This shows that they are different from another group that has different characteristics. When you examine or create a category, look for the characteristics that make the category unique. Ask yourself why the category is helpful and when you will use the category.

Radio stations earn ratings. The ratings show how much of the target audience a station has. The higher the rating, the more the station can charge to broadcast advertisements. Some stations even have "wars" to try to take listeners from each other.

Media **W**ise

Some stations change formats slightly from morning to evening. A station may be chatty and up-tempo during the day and mellow or "laid back" at night. Other stations stick to the same format day and night. Why might a station change formats? Why would a station keep the same format day and night?

Create a profile of two radio stations. Listen to the stations for at least thirty minutes and answer these questions.

1. What is each station's format?

_____

_____

2. What is the target audience for each station?

_____

_____

3. What products and services advertise on the station?

_____

_____

4. What features does the station offer listeners? For example, are there request shows or long music segments?

_____

_____

5. What is the DJ style of each show? For example, are the DJs "rapid rappers" or "mellow mikers"? Describe their chat.

_____

_____

Your Opinion

How would you rate each station? Use a scale of 1 to 5, with 1 being "poor," and 5 being "excellent." Explain your rating.

_____

_____

_____

_____

_____

_____

Lesson 2
The Power of Music as Controversy

"This hooby doopy, oopp-shoop, ottie ottie, boom boom de addy boom, scoobledy goobled dump— is trash."(1956)

"Imposed musical savagery." (1979)

"Demeaning and degrading... bowing down to the worst, most perverse desires of our enemies." (1995)

Throughout its history, music has stirred controversy. The comments above are just a few examples. People have strong feelings about what they hear. But what, exactly, are they hearing? What makes up a song? You are probably already familiar with most of these:

lyrics	What are the words to the song?
melody	What is the tune that is sung or played?
tempo	Is the song fast, slow, or in between?
rhythm	Does the song have a steady beat or an irregular beat?
performer	Who is the person or group singing the song?
instruments	What instruments are used in the song?

Controversial music has often been banned. In the 19th century, some European countries would not allow waltzes to be played. They felt the music and dances were too sensuous. In Nazi Germany, Hitler banned music by Jewish composers. This was an act of discrimination against Jewish people. In the early days of American radio, some stations refused to play music performed by African Americans. This was an example of the racism that many Americans protested in later years.

71

MEDIA WISE

The huge popularity of rock 'n' roll was helped by the invention of the 45 RPM record. These small records with the big holes in the middle were perfect for single recordings. They were lightweight. They played for about three minutes on a side and cost about $1.00. Today, most singles are sold as cassettes. Americans buy about 2 million of them a week.

Any one of these—or a combination—can make a song controversial. People who hated jazz disliked the fast tempos and strange melodies. They thought some instruments, such as the saxophone, were strange. Critics of rock 'n' roll hated the lyrics and the steady beat. They did not like the way some performers moved their bodies and banged their instruments.

Some songs are controversial because they express strong feelings. The lyrics may express anger, fear, protest, or rebellion. Some artists claim that their songs reflect problems in society.

Choose a song that you think is controversial. Then answer the questions about the song.

1. What is the name of the song?

_____

_____

2. What parts of the song are controversial? Describe the lyrics, melody, tempo, rhythm, performer, and instruments.

_____

_____

_____

_____

_____

_____

_____

_____

3. What do people who like the song say about it?

_____

_____

_____

_____

_____

_____

_____

_____

_____

_____

72

4. What do people who dislike the song say about it?

_____

_____

_____

_____

5. What issue or problem in society does the song reflect?

_____

_____

_____

_____

6. Do you think the song has had an impact on society? Will it have one? Why or why not?

_____

_____

_____

_____

_____

_____

_____

_____

DISCUSSION

Radio is a broadcast medium. Its sounds reach millions of listeners. Of course, listeners can change stations or turn off the radio. Even so, some people feel that controversial songs should not be played on radio. What do you think? In a small group, discuss your ideas. Use examples from your own experience.

Lesson 3
It's a Hit!

TOP TEN HIT LIST

1. **MARIAH CAREY AND BOYZ II MEN**
   "One Sweet Day"–Columbia
2. **WHITNEY HOUSTON**
   "Exhale (Shoop Shoop)"–Arista
3. **LL COOL J**
   "Hey Lover"–Def Jam/RAL/Island
4. **COOLIO FEATURING L.V.**
   "Gangsta's Paradise"–MCA Soundtracks
5. **TLC**
   "Diggin' On You"–LaFace/Arista
6. **THE BEATLES**
   "Free as a Bird"–Apple/Capitol
7. **DEEP BLUE SOMETHING**
   "Breakfast at Tiffany's"– Rainmaker/Interscope
8. **MARIAH CAREY**
   "Fantasy"–Columbia
9. **MONICA**
   "Before You Walk Out of My Life/Like This and Like That"–Rowdy/Arista
10. **GOO GOO DOLLS**
    "Name"–Metal Blade/Warner Bros.

"What was that song?"

"Can you please play it again?"

Most records are bought by females aged 18 to 24.

An exception to the up-tempo hit is the "summer" hit. The hit song of the summer tends to be a ballad or slow song.

In the 1950s the U.S. government began investigating record companies. Some record company executives were found guilty of paying radio DJs to play certain records. Investigations continued into the 1990s but with fewer convictions.

You probably know today's top hits. But do you know how a song becomes a hit? Several factors play a role. Record companies spend time and lots of money promoting their artists' records. A radio station's **playlist** (the list of songs played) is usually chosen by the stations's PD, or program director. The PD considers these factors:

- The track record of the artist—does the artist have "name recognition"? Do people know the artist because of an earlier hit, concerts, or videos?
- The tempo of the song—an up-tempo song is more likely to become a hit than a slow song.
- "Adult" appeal—these are themes such as love, separation, hurt, and regret. Teenagers as well as adults tend to buy records that have adult themes.
- Requests—does the record get the most requests on call-in shows?
- Music video—does the song have a hot video played on one of the television music channels?

Choose two of today's hit songs. Tell why you think each song became a hit. Use your experience from listening to radio and watching TV. Also use your knowledge of what makes up a song (lyrics, tempo, performer, and so on). Then compare your ideas with those of your classmates. On what factors do you agree? On what factors do you disagree?

Song Number One

Title:

_____

Why do you think this song became a hit?

_____

_____

_____

_____

Song Number Two

Title:

_____

Why do you think this song became a hit?

_____

_____

_____

_____

Name a new song that you think will become a hit. Tell why you think it will hit the top.

_____

_____

_____

_____

_____

_____

_____

The real money in recordings is in album sales. Americans buy almost 10 million albums a week. Most album sales are CDs.

Program Director for a Day

Suppose you are the person in control of a radio station for a day. You can shape the station's programming for 24 hours. Use the categories below to describe the choices you will make on a separate sheet.

FORMAT

STATION ID (Write what the announcers would say to introduce the radio station.)

AUDIENCE (Describe the demographics.)

SONGS to be played

FEATURES (Describe each one you'd have: news, weather, traffic, contests, call-ins, and so on)

DJs you would use and why

PROMOTIONS (How would you get people to listen to your station? Describe give-aways and contests you would have.)

Unit Test

Checking What You Have Learned

1. Each of the four phrases below could be used to complete the following statement. Circle the best choice. Explain your choice on the lines provided.

   Music has the power to

       a. change the world.   c. annoy people in the next room.

       b. stir up controversy.   d. settle disagreements.

   _____

   _____

2. Mark with an *X* the statement that is true. Explain your choice on the lines provided.

   ❑ Categories help you organize information.

   ❑ Characteristics in one category should overlap with those in another.

   _____

   _____

3. Why is catching and keeping an audience a hard job for a radio station?

   _____

   _____

4. What factors contribute to the making of a hit record? Answer this essay question on a separate sheet of paper. Give examples to support your answer.

Checking How You Learned

Use the following questions to evaluate your performance in this unit.
   - What did you learn about different categories of music stations?
   - Were you able to describe the controversy about a particular song? If not, what can you do to recognize why a song might be controversial?
   - What did you learn about how a recording becomes a hit?

Getting the Messages from Audio Media

Audio media is everywhere and just about everyone has some contact with it. The United States has 10,000 radio stations. Most of these stations broadcast talk shows and music to millions of listeners. People listen to recorded music at home, and in their car. Portable players allow people to listen to music anywhere. Americans spend billions of dollars each year on recorded music.

In Unit 1, you learned about information radio. You learned that some programs have hosts who are experts on a certain topic. They give information and respond to questions from callers. You learned that some of these hosts also give commercial announcements for products that sponsor their shows.

In Unit 2, you learned about "inflammation" radio. You learned that hosts on these shows give their opinions on different topics. They take calls from listeners who also give their own opinions. You learned that some talk show hosts can be biased in their opinions.

In Unit 3, you learned about music recordings. You learned about different categories of music played on radio. You learned that music has the power to create controversy. You also learned some of the factors that go into making a hit record.

For this project, you will design your own survey to find out how people are influenced by different kinds of audio media. You will conduct your survey and summarize the results. Then you will present your results to the class.

STEP 1

Designing the Survey.......

Work in a small group to plan your survey. When you take a survey, you want to find out what a large number of people think about a certain issue. To reach this goal, you need to design a survey form. The form includes questions that people will answer.

With your group, brainstorm the kinds of information you want to find out. Use the survey plan on the following page. Some factors you might consider include the following:

- What age groups listen to audio media?
- How many hours a day do people listen to the radio?
- How many hours do people listen to information radio?
- How many hours do people listen to "inflammation" radio?
- How many hours do people listen to music on the radio?
- At what times of day do people listen?
- Do people listen to a certain station or host for a special reason?
- How does the program affect their mood?

Your survey form should ask the questions. It should also have room for people to respond to each question. Some responses may take more room than others. Plan your survey form so that it fits on one sheet of paper. The form below has some sample questions that you can use to start your survey. Invent at least four more questions that deal directly with the issue your group has chosen to study.

AUDIO MEDIA SURVEY

Your age: _____

Please answer these questions.

1. How many hours a day do you spend listerning to the radio?
   _____ hours.

2. What is your favorite kind of program? Check one.
   ❏ information show   ❏ opinion show   ❏ music show

   Why? _____
   _____

3. At what time of day do you usually listen to the radio?
   ❏ morning   ❏ afternoon   ❏ evening

STEP 2 Gathering Information...

Survey the people. Decide how you will get people to respond to your survey. Will you personally hand them a copy? Will you call people and ask them questions over the phone? Decide how many people you want to fill out survey forms. You should have one copy of the form for each person.

Next, figure out how much time it will take to complete the survey. How many people will each person in your group talk to? Try not to take more than 10 minutes of a person's time.

STEP 3 Analyzing the Results......

Collect all your surveys and tabulate the results. You can use any method to summarize your data. The following chart is a sample. Add new categories or design your own chart.

Total Hours of Listening	
Hours Listening to Information Radio	
Hours Listening to "Inflammation" Radio	
Hours Listening to Music Radio	
Favorite Listening Times	

Now you are ready to analyze the results. Here are some questions to discuss with your group. After the discussion, you should be ready to present your report.

- What was the most surprising information we found?
- What was the least surprising information we found?
- What did we learn from the information?
- Do we have all the information we need?
- Based on the information, what conclusion can we draw about the effects of audio media on listeners?

STEP 4 Preparing and Presenting the Results ••••••••••••••••••

Work with your group. Use the forms you made and your answers to the questions in Step 3. Use the following outline to summarize the information.

- Tell how many people you surveyed and how you gathered the information.
- Present your findings. Use the words and numbers from your forms. You might begin, "We found that X number of people listen to....."
- Give your analysis of the information. Describe the conclusions your group made from the survey. Present your group report to the class. Ask your classmates if they have any questions or comments regarding your report.

STEP 5

Evaluating the Report ••••

As you listen to other groups give their reports, offer supportive comments. Compliment them on one step of the project. Use the following checklist to evaluate the reports.

Did the report include the following points:
- A description (the aim of the survey and how many people were surveyed)
- A clear summary (the number of people who listen to each category of audio media, the number of hours people listen, the effects the programs have on people, and so on)
- An analysis (what your group learned, what conclusions you made from the information)

PART 3

FOCUS ON TELEVISION AND MOVIES

On **September 8, 1966,** a new show named *Star Trek* was aired on TV. This show was an outer space adventure. It was not a hit right away. In fact, it went off the air after three years. Yet its audience kept growing. People watched reruns of the shows. They wrote in to ask for another TV series. Since 1966, there have been three new TV series and many *Star Trek* films produced. Around the world, people know that Klingons are characters from *Star Trek*. Most people know that "beam me up" is a *Star Trek* command. *Star Trek* is part of our culture.

Why are some movies and TV shows so long-lasting? Partly, because they tell exciting stories. More than that, though, they bring viewers into another world. Viewers can visit faraway places and even other time zones. They can "meet" interesting people. They can watch people face danger without facing danger themselves. In a tough world, they can see as many happy endings as they like.

Movies were created in the 1890s. The first movies were a few minutes long. They had no sound. By 1912, films told full-length stories. By 1927, they had sound. Television came along in the late

1940s. Today, both the movie and TV industries are huge businesses. Hit films can earn over $150 million in ticket sales. TV captures millions of viewers because it can offer hundreds of channels. We are in the middle of an entertainment explosion.

PROGRAMMING Most films and TV programs are made to entertain audiences. Entertainment shows on TV include weekly series, sports shows, and music videos.

Documentaries are factual films about a subject. They are usually made to inform audiences.

Television information shows include newscasts and how-to programs. Of course, informative shows try to entertain, too. They want to keep viewers interested.

AUDIENCE Almost everyone in the United States watches a movie or television program every week. Over 20 million people go to the movies each week. Over 100 million people might watch TV on a given night. Each week, about 20 million people tune in to music channels like MTV.

FUNDING Most TV is funded by advertising. Advertisers air commercials during programs. They pay a fee to do this. A 30-second commercial on a hit show can cost from $300,000 to $500,000. A show can make over $3 million a week from commercials.

Some cable stations also air commercials. Also, cable viewers pay monthly fees to receive cable signals in their homes.

Public television stations receive their funds from the government. They also receive contributions from viewers and businesses.

IMPACT Movies and TV have changed American culture. To many people, they *are* American culture. Movies and TV shows are among the best-known American exports. Darth Vader, Mickey Mouse, and Big Bird are famous around the world.

Movies and TV are big business. Some of the world's largest companies are entertainment companies. This means that a big part of what goes on in the business world has to do with movies and TV.

CRITICAL ISSUES Many people worry about the content of movies, TV shows, and music videos. They say that these media stress sex and violence. TV is a special worry to some people. Because TV beams its programs right into homes, anything on TV can easily reach young children.

Some people worry about who controls TV and movies. Huge companies are buying up most of the TV networks and film-making businesses. For example, the Walt Disney Company now owns ABC, parts of four cable channels, twenty-one radio stations, and a book publisher. Fewer and fewer people are deciding what more and more of us read, see, hear, and buy. Will this limit the free spread of ideas in the future?

In Part 3, you will examine issues that have to do with TV and movies.

► A network is a system of television stations. A network supplies programs to member stations. Examples of American networks are NBC, CBS, ABC, and Fox. How much power do you think networks have over what you get to watch on television?

► Advertisers pay for a TV show by buying commercial time during the show. They use this time to advertise their products. It costs more to buy commercial time during a popular show. This is because more viewers are watching so the product will get wide exposure.

► Advertisers and networks have several tools for finding out about program audiences. One is market research. This research breaks down an audience by age, sex, how much they earn, and so on. Another tool is ratings. Ratings are a measure of how many people are watching a program. How might each of these tools be useful to advertisers?

The AFA TV network building is open late tonight. Tiger Hansen's office is full of papers, soda cans, and half-eaten sandwiches. Hansen is AFA's programming chief. He and his assistants, Zelda Oakley and Melvin Drake, are planning the new season's nighttime schedule. All of AFA's channels will broadcast these shows.

Programming for prime time is a huge job. **Prime time** is the hours between 8 p.m. and 11 p.m. On Sundays, prime time starts at 7 p.m. These are the hours when the greatest numbers of people watch TV. Networks charge more money to air commercials during prime time shows.

Right now, the programming team is thinking about weekly comedy and drama series. Weekly series are the backbone of any TV schedule. The team must decide which old series to keep. They must also choose new shows to add.

Tiger Hansen says, "Of course we'll keep *What a Family*. It's still one of America's five most-watched shows."

Zelda Oakley frowns. "Remember, Rob Taggart wants an extra $100,000 an episode." Rob Taggart is the popular star of *What a Family*. He already earns $250,000 for each weekly episode.

"He'll get the raise," says Melvin Drake. "He's worth it. We make more than $300,000 from one 30-second commercial during his show. He really pulls in advertisers."

"Fine," says Oakley. "What about *Detection Connection?*"

Hansen shakes his head. "It's not big with the 18-to-49 age group. That's who advertisers want. Most people who watch *Detection Connection* are over 60. Besides, detective shows are on their way out. The big thing today is comedies. The 18-to-49 group wants comedies with good-looking young people. The characters should be neighbors and have glamorous jobs. The other networks each have at least three shows like that. We only have one."

Drake looks at a list. "You mean *21 Chevron Road*. It's moving up fast in the ratings. The stars are catching on with fans."

"Sounds good," says Hansen. "We need more than one comedy with good-looking neighbors, though."

"There are three among the new shows," says Oakley. "In one, good-looking young doctors live in a high-rise in Honolulu. In another, good-looking young politicians share a townhouse near Washington, D.C. In the third, a team of good-looking young superheroes lives in a hidden stronghold in Roswell, New Mexico."

"Terrific," says Hansen. "We'll watch their pilots again. Then we'll choose two of them."

Oakley looks at a list. "Now, what about *Doctors on Duty?*"

Hansen says, "We definitely keep it. Advertisers love it. Its viewers are mostly young. Most of them have high-paying jobs. They spend a lot of money on cars, computers, travel, and sports equipment."

"What a terrific show," says Drake. He rolls his eyes.

One hour is still empty in the schedule. Oakley says, "We have two choices left: *Cosmic Zappers* and *On Our Block*."

"Oh, no," says Hansen. He has to weigh the two programs. *Cosmic Zappers* is a new show. It is based on a hit movie. The movie has brought in $215 million in ticket sales. In addition, kids and teen-agers have bought millions of *Cosmic Zapper* action figures and video games.

On the other hand, *On Our Block* has been praised by critics for years. It is beautifully written. The actors have won awards year after year. Ratings are not high, though. Another network has dropped the show. AFA has the chance to pick it up.

"It's a huge risk," says Hansen. "Of course, *M*A*S*H* was a risk at the beginning. In the end, it lasted eleven years."

"Let's not forget *Hill Street Blues*, *Picket Fences*, and *Star Trek*," says Oakley.

"Critics will love this show even if ratings are low," says Hansen. "Critical praise always makes a network look good."

"*Cosmic Zappers*, though, will make lots of ad money," says Drake. "So what's your decision, boss?"

"I need to think about this," says Hansen.

Drake and Oakley sigh. This is going to be a long night.

A **pilot** is like a sample show of a series. Pilots are made to sell shows to networks.

Suppose you are a network programmer. You notice that another network's science fiction adventure series is the top-rated show. You want your network's programs to earn high ratings. Would you be likely to program a science fiction adventure series too? Networks risk a lot of money on new shows. They prefer to plan a show that is a "sure thing". This may mean using an idea that is already successful. Or it may mean casting a popular star.

Which program do you think Tiger Hansen will choose? Why? Which would you choose? Why?

Lesson 1
In Search of Real Life on TV

Sometimes TV seems like a huge treasure chest. It shows every kind of experience you can imagine. You can watch brave lifeguards make dramatic rescues. You can share family life with a rich, handsome, funny family. You can be part of the glamorous world of a big city. TV is a great place to visit. But do you ever think you live there?

Most TV shows fall into a few basic categories. These include news shows, talk shows, comedies, dramas, and sports shows. The two main categories of shows that tell a story are dramas and comedies.

MEDIA WISE

A **story line** or **plot** is the series of events that happens in a comedy or drama. A plot usually has an ending, or **outcome.** Events are tied up neatly. All problems are solved. Other shows have continuing story lines. In these shows, an episode might end with a **cliffhanger.** This is a surprising event that makes viewers want to tune in to the next episode. How do you think neat outcomes and cliffhangers compare with real life? Why do you think such endings are satisfying in a TV show?

Know Your Shows

Dramas: These usually have serious or exciting story lines. Their endings may be happy or sad. The heroes usually do not die in the end. A drama may be set in a hospital, a police station, a small town, or even outer space. An episode of a drama show is usually at least one hour long.

Comedies: A comedy may also be called a **situation comedy** or **sitcom.** In a comedy, characters do funny things to make funny things happen. Some sitcoms take up serious ideas like divorce. Usually, though, the situation is light. Many comedies are filmed before an audience. The audience's laughter becomes part of the show. Some comedies have a **laugh track**--recorded laughter that plays after each joke. Sitcoms are usually shorter than dramas. An episode is usually thirty minutes long.

With your group, play a word association game. Put a checkmark by the words in light type that best describe the word in bold. On the following line, write other words you think of to describe the bold word.

1. **doctor** ❑ handsome/beautiful ❑ tall ❑ does lots of paperwork

_____

2. **old person** ❑ forgetful ❑ rude ❑ goes to work every day

_____

3. **hero** ❏ handsome/beautiful ❏ strong ❏ bald

_____

4. **straight A student** ❏ funny-looking ❏ unpopular ❏ athletic

_____

5. **people in love** ❏ young ❏ good-looking ❏ rude

_____

Did anyone check the third item in each row? That is what many doctors, older people, and so on are like in real life. You could not tell from most TV shows! TV programs often show people as **stereotypes.** Stereotypes are easy for a writer to write about. Because TV episodes are only 30 or 60 minutes long, there is not much time to develop a character fully. Stereotypes are easy for viewers to understand quickly. Viewers will get drawn into a show right away because they will identify the stereotypical characters and they will be less likely to change the channel.

Some stereotypes from TV shows are listed on this page. With your group, try to name one or two shows that have characters like this.

Bratty younger brother or sister

_____

Best friend who always says stupid things

_____

Dad who always says or does goofy things

_____

Bad guy with bad hair, skin, or teeth

_____

Bad guy with a regional accent (Southern, Brooklyn)

_____

Woman who screams in dangerous situations

_____

Handsome guy who always succeeds

_____

What other familiar stereotypes can you think of from TV?

_____

Of course, a TV drama probably could *not* show all possible real-life traits and events. For example, showing a doctor doing hours of paperwork is poor storytelling. Viewers should remember that TV often gives a glamorous or incomplete view of life.

Watch an episode of three different TV programs. Two should be sitcoms about families. One should be a drama. Use the following list to help you evaluate what you see.

- Think about the way the main characters are shown.
- Time all commercial breaks (series of commercials). Write down the total amount of time of each commercial break.
- Keep a tally of the number of commercials shown in each commercial break.
- Try to figure out how the episode will end.

After you watch the shows, answer the following questions on a separate sheet of paper.

List the three shows you watched.

1. In general, what traits did the male main characters have for each show?

2. In general, what traits did the female main characters have?

3. Were any people shown who were disabled, very ugly, or poorly dressed? If so, what were the characters like?

4. What was the total amount of time used for commercials?

5. What were you able to predict about the plot?

6. Do any of these shows present a realistic view of life? Explain your answer.

DISCUSSION

Suppose you lived in another country. The only thing you knew about the United States was through watching American TV comedies and dramas and commercials. What would you think a typical American family is like? What are typical American jobs? How do typical American parents behave? How do teenagers behave? How do young adults behave? What problems do you think that a television view of the United States might cause?

Lesson 2
A Vote for Me Is a Vote for America

A lot of political campaign money is spent on TV ads. In the 1994 elections, one candidate for the U.S. Senate spent over $25 million on his campaign. How could anyone possibly spend that much running for office? Campaign ads are just one way that TV plays a part in how we vote.

Most people agree that the first "TV president" was John F. Kennedy. In 1960, he ran against Richard Nixon. The two men agreed to have a series of debates on TV.

In the first debate, Nixon looked thin, tired, and sweaty. He seemed ill at ease. Kennedy looked young, fit, and relaxed. He answered questions with confidence. Many people think that those debates gave Kennedy an edge in the election. Politicians have been paying attention to television ever since.

Today, politicians know how to use TV to their advantage. Here are some of the ways.

- Politicians hold press conferences. These conferences may be shown on TV.
- Mayors, governors, and especially the President will sometimes give a speech about an important issue or event.
- Politicians appear on news shows such as *Face the Nation* or *Meet the Press.* These shows deal with the current issues or events of the day.
- Candidates run ads that say bad things about other candidates.
- Candidates go on talk shows or appear on MTV. This helps them reach young voters.
- Candidates hold debates. A debate lets the voter compare the candidates side by side.

Politicians want their viewpoints and personalities to appeal to voters. To do this, politicians often consult advertising and marketing experts.

Two politicians are running against each other. Each one has something to say about taxes. Read their TV speeches below.

Politician 1:

We Americans should be able to keep more of the money we earn. Why should we work just to pay the government? The government is a huge bottomless stomach. It gobbles up our hard-earned money. We

Near election time, candidates air their TV ads. An ad may cost tens of thousands of dollars *each time* it airs. An ad may air dozens of times in a week. Why do you think candidates spend so much money on these TV ads?

By law, radio and TV stations must allow time for an opposing view when the President gives a speech. This means that a spokesperson from the other party can give a speech too. There are other equal-time laws that deal with candidates. Why do you think these laws were made?

THE LANGUAGE OF THINKING

As you have already learned, a **fact** is an actual event or true information. An **opinion** is a belief based on someone's judgment. People often support their opinions with facts. However, they can choose facts cleverly so that their opinions look sound. For example, many facts may be known about a particular event. A politician might mention only the facts that support his or her opinion. How could you learn the facts that the politician does *not* tell you?

don't need the government deciding how to spend our money. We can make those decisions better ourselves. If taxpayers pay lower taxes, they'll spend that money in the community. Stores and other businesses will make more money. These businesses will hire more workers. Lower taxes could solve the jobs problem in this country!

Politician 2:

Whenever we lower taxes, the rich always get the biggest tax break. That's why they love tax cuts so much. Meanwhile, important government programs are closed down. These programs help all of us. They fund crimefighting, schools, and road repairs. We may think we're saving money by cutting taxes. No—we're actually losing in the long run. Do you want fewer police on our streets? Do you want your kids to be crammed into overcrowded classrooms? Do you want to drive your car across crumbling bridges? That's what lower taxes will mean.

Answer the following questions about the speeches.

1. What facts does each politician give in the speech?

   _____

2. Are these facts enough for you to make a decision about tax cuts? Why or why not?

   _____

3. What does your answer to Question 2 tell you about TV's usefulness as the only source of information about political issues?

   _____

4. What information could you get from a newspaper or magazine that you did not get from these speeches?

   _____

MEDIA WISE

TV ads and programs are geared to carry quick messages. Advertisers and programmers want to grab viewers fast before they turn to another channel. Quick messages tend to be simple and general. To get a quick message across, a politician may use a catchy phrase or a slogan. The politician hopes that the slogan will stick in viewers' minds long after the ad is over. What political slogans have you heard from TV or other sources?

Lesson 3
And Now a Late-Breaking Story

Ask a few adults what important public events they remember. They might name the shooting of President Kennedy, the first moon landing, and the 1995 Oklahoma City bombing. Ask how they learned details about these events. Nearly everyone will say, "From TV." Television delivers news instantly. TV also allows the whole world to share important experiences.

Changes in technology have changed the news. News shows of the 1940s did not report live from the scene of an event. No one could get to the scene in time for the news show. Some of these reports were even taken right from newspapers.

Today, cameras and sound equipment are lightweight and easy to handle. Jet travel is faster. Communications satellites are in use. These satellites send radio and TV signals across the world in seconds. For the first time, people can watch faraway events as they happen.

Today, there are many kinds of TV news programs. Some of them are listed here:

- Local and national news broadcasts
- News bulletins/special coverage of events
- Network morning news/talk shows: example—*Good Morning America*
- Interviews/ news analysis shows: examples—*Meet the Press, Face the Nation, Nightline*
- Weekly news magazine shows: examples—*60 Minutes, 20/20*
- Tabloid news shows: examples—*Hard Copy, Inside Edition*

Once, TV networks thought of news as a public service. Today, though, news shows compete for ratings just like other shows. This causes news shows to look for ways to make the news exciting. Some people worry that this approach blurs the line between news and entertainment.

In Part 1, you read that newspapers print both hard news and soft news. Soft news includes human interest stories. Television news programs also broadcast both hard and soft news. Today even network news shows have human-interest segments on lifestyle trends or interesting people.

MEDiA WiSE

As you learned in Part 1, a tabloid is a newspaper that prints more dramatic stories. In the same way, tabloid news shows stress stories about crime and scandal. The shows exaggerate the shocking elements of the stories. Why do you think such shows are aired? How popular do you think they are?

MEDIA WISE

In a news analysis show or news interview show, people discuss current events or issues. An entire program might center on just one or two issues. An issue can be explored in great depth. Such programs are sometimes called "talking heads" shows. This is because they consist mostly of people talking. There is no scenery, movement, or fancy camera work. Network talking head shows are usually aired on Sunday morning or late at night. Why do you think this is?

Watch one of each of these kinds of news shows:
- a weekday network evening news show
- a news analysis show or news interview show such as *Meet the Press* or *Face the Nation*
- a news magazine show such as *20/20*

Use the questions below to help you evaluate the shows.

1. About how much of the news on this program is hard news? About how much is soft news?

   Evening news: _____

   Analysis/interview show: _____

   Magazine show: _____

2. To what degree are "jazzy" elements like computer graphics, fancy camera work, or music used?

   Evening news: _____

   Analysis/interview show: _____

   Magazine show: _____

3. What kind of facts or details does the program give on its subjects?

   Evening news: _____

   Analysis/interview show: _____

   Magazine show: _____

4. Which program gives the most in-depth treatment of a subject? What techniques does this program use?

   Evening news: _____

   Analysis/interview show: _____

   Magazine show: _____

   Compare your findings with those of your classmates. What can you conclude about TV news programs as a source of information?

Lesson 4
TV Nation

"Children are taken across the globe before we give them permission to cross the street."—Joshua Meyrowitz, TV expert

"The problem with television in this country is that commercial television makes so much money doing its worst, it can't afford to do its best."—Fred Friendly, TV executive

People have been arguing about TV's influence since TV began. Some people say it has had only bad effects on us. Other people point to many good effects. Everyone agrees that, good or bad, TV's influence is strong. It has changed us in small ways and large ones.

Just think of the fads that TV has started or spread. Work with a small group. In the columns below, list fads from TV you have followed or know about.

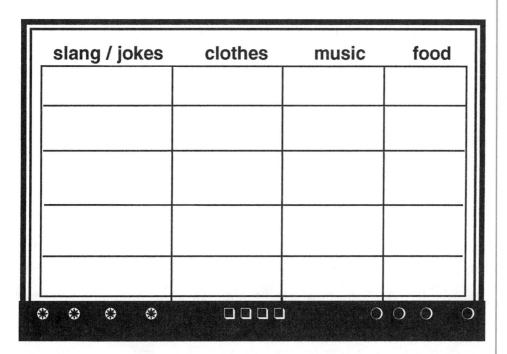

slang / jokes	clothes	music	food

Plan a debate with your group. The subject is *Has TV had a good influence or a bad influence on American society?* Divide into two small groups. One group will argue that TV has had good effects on society. The other group will argue that TV has had bad effects. Use the ideas listed below to help you prepare. Think of specific examples that support each idea on the list. Also look back at the quotes that start this lesson. Think of other ideas to explore for your argument, too. Write down what you think of so you keep it in mind.

Studies show that children and teenagers watch about twenty-two hours of TV a week. What other activities do you do for as much as twenty-two hours a week? Is there anything you could do for twenty-two hours a week that would not have an effect on you?

Product placement is a way to display products in TV shows or movies. Here is how it works. Suppose a TV program shows a kitchen scene. On the breakfast table is a box of a popular cereal. That cereal company has probably paid about $5,000 to get its product "placed" on camera. Product placement is also why your favorite TV character carries a certain brand of shampoo out of the bathroom. Companies want you to connect their brands with your favorite shows and stars. Do you use some of the same products as your favorite stars?

Good effects:

- What examples of informational TV programs have you seen?
- What faraway places have you seen on TV that you would not be able to see in real life?
- What has TV taught you about other cultures and about nature?
- What have you learned about current events from TV?
- What TV shows have made you use your imagination?
- What shows have made you want to learn more about something?

Bad effects:

- What stereotypes do you see on TV?
- What commercials have tempted you to buy or eat things you didn't really want?
- Does watching TV make you feel you are not beautiful enough, thin enough, or rich enough to have a good life?
- Do children you know seem to copy behavior they see on TV? Is some of this behavior rude or violent?

Give both groups a turn to speak without interruption. Afterwards, work individually to answer these questions.

1. Which points in the debate seemed most convincing to you?

_____

_____

2. Overall, has TV had a good influence or a bad influence on your life? Explain your answer.

_____

_____

3. Overall, has TV had a good influence or a bad influence on American life? Explain your answer.

_____

_____

4. How can you watch TV more critically to increase its good effects on you and lessen its bad effects?

_____

_____

Studies show that by age 12, most children have seen about 101,000 acts of violence on TV. Of these, about 13,000 are murders. Many experts believe that TV violence leads to real violence. After seeing all that violence, kids—and adults—become used to it. It becomes no big deal. Do you think this is possible? How might you learn enough to decide?

Look at the TV You Watch

In this activity, you will examine your TV viewing habits. Work with a group of classmates. Follow these steps:

- Gather the TV listings for an entire week. These could be from a TV magazine or your local newspaper.

- Examine the listings. On a separate sheet of paper, write down all the shows you have watched during the past week. Include movies you watched on video. Then fill in the following lines.

    Number of programs I watched: _____

    Number of hours of TV I watched: _____

- Discuss each of the following questions with your group. Then write your answers on a separate sheet.

1. What is the range of hours that people in your class spend watching TV each week? What is the average weekly number of hours that people in your class watch?

2. Compare this with the hours per week that you spend in classes (not including lunch or after-school activities). Which number is greater? By how much?

3. Think about the last time you watched TV. Recall the programs and commercials you saw. What details stick most clearly in your mind? Do you feel better off in any way because you remember these details?

4. What benefits do you think you got from TV during the week?

5. Think about programs you watch regularly. Could you choose one program to recommend to someone else because of its high quality? This program does not have to be an educational show. You could choose a comedy or drama series that is well-written and well-produced. Give your reasons for choosing the show you chose. If you *cannot* pick a show, tell how you decided that none of the shows measured up.

Unit Test

Checking What You Have Learned

1. Most TV news shows feature either all hard news or all soft news.—State whether you agree or disagree. Explain your reasons.

   _____

   _____

2. Put an *X* next to the statement that is true. Explain your choice on the lines provided.

   ❑ TV programmers tend to choose shows that are likely to be popular with viewers between the ages of 18 and 49.

   ❑ Politicians try to give a fair, balanced view of issues in their campaign ads.

   _____

   _____

3. Advertisers pay less to air commercials on low-rated shows. Yet most advertisers would rather buy expensive commercial time on high-rated shows. Why? Give examples to support your answer.

   _____

   _____

4. Explain at least three ways in which TV influences the way people think or act. Answer the essay question on a separate sheet of paper. Give examples to support your answer.

Checking How You Learned

Use the following questions to evaluate your performance in this unit.
- What did you learn about the way ratings affect what is shown on TV?
- What did you learn about how to evaluate different kinds of news programs as information sources?
- What did you learn about evaluating TV shows to see how closely they reflect real life?

Advertising on Television

Advertisers want to reach people who will buy their products. That is why companies spend over *$20 billion* a year on TV ads. They know that 98 percent of U.S. homes have at least one TV set. The average set may be on for six or seven hours a day. In that time, a single station may run over 100 commercials. Millions of people watch these commercials.

Years ago, commercials were often 60 seconds long. Then 30-second ads became common. In the past ten years, 15-second commercials have become popular. As a result, viewers are seeing more commercials than ever before.

So many commercials often cause confusion. Viewers cannot recall most of the ads they see. Sometimes they remember the commercial, but not the product.

Hitting the Target

Suppose you want to sell SugarWhammo Bubblegum. Would you show your commercial late at night? Or, would you run it Saturday morning? Why?

Advertisers try to gauge the best time to run their commercials. They look for shows that appeal to their target audience. For instance, a company that sells make-up will advertise during shows that women like. Even the best commercial cannot sell products to an audience that does not use their product.

The most popular shows have the largest audiences. Networks charge higher prices for air time on these shows. Special shows are the most costly. Thirty seconds of commercial time on a major sports event can cost over half a million dollars! Advertisers pay because they can reach huge numbers of viewers. Spending a half million is worth it if a commercial gains five million in sales.

Tricks of the Trade

Advertisers study their target audience. They tailor commercials to specific viewers. They consider the age and sex of the audience. They study viewer likes and dislikes. For example, while teens may like a commercial with background rock music, older viewers probably would not like it.

Commercials use color, sound, and special effects. Each commercial has its own mood and pace. A commercial for Mother's Day flowers may blend soft colors with calm music. A car commercial may show red cars zooming through clouds. The music may be loud and fast.

Advertisers want you to remember their product's name. The name may flash on the TV screen many times. Actors may say the name over and over. A song or jingle may repeat the name. How else do commercials help you remember product names?

Getting Through to You

Commercials use many methods to sell products. Some are the same as those you have read about for print media and radio.

One favorite is the **scientific claim.** Scientific claims use facts and figures to try to impress you. Others use fancy words. Yet the claim may have little real meaning. Here are some examples:

New Blast cleanser removes 37 percent more dirt! Great. Thirty-seven percent more than what?

Fresheroo toothpaste sweetens your breath with benzyldane. What is "benzyldane"? Is Fresheroo the only toothpaste that has it?

Researchers have spent years testing PainBeGone tablets. So what? All medicines must undergo testing.

Some commercials take the **wishes-come-true** approach. Use this product, the ad says, and your problem is solved. Here is an example.

Two teenage girls are standing in front of a mirror. "My hair is so limp," says one girl. "Mike will never ask me to the dance."

Her friend smiles. She hands her a bottle. "Here. Try Starbreak shampoo."

Can you guess the last scene? Of course. The girl is dancing with Mike. Her hair is gorgeous. Problem solved. Her wish has come true.

Some commercials do not *seem* to be selling a product. They seem to be informing you. But such **infomercials** are really just paid ads. They use facts to sell their product.

Infomercials are often used to "sell" candidates to voters. Suppose Pam Greene is running for mayor. An infomercial may describe the city's problems. Next, it may discuss Greene's many skills. Then it might tell what Greene plans to do. The infomercial may look like a news story. Yet it is really just a commercial.

Answer the following questions about TV commercials.

1. Describe a commercial you have seen that uses one or more of the methods discussed. Include details like the product name, the use of color and sound, the time that the commercial was shown, the program it interrupted, and the possible target audience.

   _____

   _____

2. Car makers run ads in print media, on radio, and on TV. Why do you think they advertise in different kinds of media? What other products are advertised in more than one place?

   _____

   _____

In the early 1980s people smirked at cable TV. They thought it was just a tacky fad. "Why bother?", they asked. In 1981, Warner Cable began showing music videos twenty-four hours a day. People said it would never last. That was in the early 1980s.

Fifteen years later, cable television lives. Some people might even say cable TV "rules." Dozens of channels earn hundreds of millions of dollars from advertisers. And music on television? The MTV channel alone is watched by 58 million households. The channel is picked up in over seventy countries around the world. Yet MTV is only one of several cable channels that now plays music videos. These music video channels are among the most influential on television.

Beginnings

Music videos were first shown in dance clubs in Europe. They were intended to promote record sales of new music groups. Cable executives saw the chance for something new. They liked the idea of a kind of radio station with pictures.

In its early days, music television was just that. Video jockeys (VJs) announced and played videos. Video after video played, twenty-four hours a day. The early videos were all pop or rock. The great majority of the videos were by white artists. Then in 1988,

MTV's biggest show is the annual Video Music Awards. In 1994, 58 million households saw the show. In 1995, 61 million tuned in. That is just in the United States. World-wide, about 300 million people saw the show. Why do you suppose advertisers are interested in these figures?

Music videos quickly took a leading edge in film technique. Commercials and movies were quick to adopt the fast paced style created for music videos.

MTV started a rap program. Other programming changes came soon after.

THE MAKING OF A MUSIC VIDEO

Music videos are really short movies. They use many of the same methods that are used to make movies. These are the typical steps in making a music video:

- A musician or group records a song.
- A producer and director come up with ideas for a video.
- A script writer prepares a script for the video. The script shows who will perform in the video. It describes the locations, scenes, and main camera shots of the video.
- A choreographer plans the dances and teaches them to the performers.
- The director guides the performers in rehearsing their parts.
- Make-up, costumes, and special effects are created.
- Cameras record each scene. There may be hundreds of "takes" or filmed segments.
- The director, producer, and film editor work together to mix the final video. The visual images on film must be synchronized or "synched" with the soundtrack. Special effects, animation, and additional soundtracks may be added. The final video may have hundreds or thousands of "cuts." These are changes in the video image—a different camera angle or another scene. The number and speed of the cuts help give the video its pace and style.

Lesson 1
What Is Playing on Music Television?

Most viewers tune into music video channels for the music videos. Yet viewers want something more than just videos. One channel announced that it was going to put "music first." It boosted music videos to fill 90 percent of its air time. Viewers began tuning out. The station's ratings dropped. So it added other programs besides music videos.

Today's music video channels also offer a variety of programs. Among the most popular shows are cartoons or 'toons. These include toon adventures and situation comedies. Another popular category is the real-life situation. The camera records real people in a situation. Two of the most popular real-life shows have been "Real World" and "Road Rules"

Some channels offer news programs. They also have celebrity interviews, game shows, and sports shows.

How Does a Video Become a Hit?

One major music channel has a "Buzz-Bin." It includes videos that the channel executives think have a chance of becoming hits. These videos are played—or "rotated"—often. Some channels have call-in shows. Viewers pay to call in and vote for their favorite video. Videos that get the most calls get played the most.

◀ Music video channels live for ratings. In this way, they are just like other channels. The ratings show the popularity of certain shows and of the whole channel. High ratings attract big advertisers and big bucks.

◀ MTV's *Beavis and Butthead* began in May of 1993. It became the most successful show in the channel's history. The two characters are stupid, sometimes violent, rude, and selfish. But viewers enjoy laughing at them, and laughing with them.

Seventy-five percent of the videos in MTV's Buzz Bin reach gold or platinum. (That's one or two million copies sold). The Box is another music channel. It has call-in segments. Some record executives have been accused of "jacking The Box". They are said to pay people to call in and vote for a certain video.

1. Conduct a class poll. Find out which shows and videos on music television are the most popular. List your four favorites, then work with other members of your class. Make a master list of all the programs and videos students named. Count the votes each one received. Which are the most popular? Discuss why these shows and videos are the most popular.

2. Plan your own 24-hour music video schedule. Use the hour outline below. Name the kind of program or videos you would show during that hour. You may repeat segments the way real channels do.

12:00 A.M. _____ (midnight)	**12:00 P.M.** _____ (noon)
1:00 A.M. _____	**1:00 P.M.** _____
2:00 A.M. _____	**2:00 P.M.** _____
3:00 A.M. _____	**3:00 P.M.** _____
4:00 A.M. _____	**4:00 P.M.** _____
5:00 A.M. _____	**5:00 P.M.** _____
6:00 A.M. _____	**6:00 P.M.** _____
7:00 A.M. _____	**7:00 P.M.** _____
8:00 A.M. _____	**8:00 P.M.** _____
9:00 A.M. _____	**9:00 P.M.** _____
10:00 A.M. _____	**10:00 P.M.** _____
11:00 A.M. _____	**11:00 P.M.** _____

DISCUSSION

• •

Some critics do not like the nonmusic shows on music channels. They complain that the shows are shallow and boring. They say, "Who wants to watch a bunch of teens on a camping trip?" Another complaint is, "How does this show help teens learn about real life?" Discuss the value of nonmusic shows that deal with teenagers. Support your opinions with reasons and examples.

Lesson 2
Who Watches Music Television?

Ummm...Ahhh...Delicious!

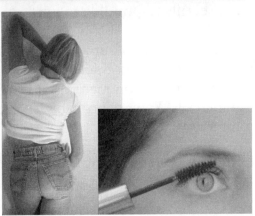

Music television has a unique audience. Its viewers are almost all under the age of 34. This includes a group that advertisers call "Generation Y." People in this group are aged 13 to 19. There are about 27 million teenagers in this group. Generation Y has grown up with TV and computers. It is the generation of the nineties.

Music channels love these viewers. To get and keep viewers, music channels have several strategies. These include the following:

- Up-beat, attractive VJs and hosts.
- Special-interest program segments (Some examples are Top-20, alternative rock, contests, and nonmusic programs.) Most channels play 15- to 30-minute segments of videos. Then they play 5 to 10 minutes of commercials. Regular segments tend to keep viewers tuned in and advertisers prefer tuned-in audiences.
- Promotional announcements for the channel—VJs and hosts tell viewers what's coming up next. They make the coming attractions seem exciting and tell viewers, "Don't go away!" or "Stay tuned!"

Advertisers work hard to create zap-resistant commercials. They want commercials to be quick and cool. And most commercials on music channels are just that way. The standard commercial is 15 seconds long, with at least seven "cuts," or changes in the camera shot. The commercials use many of the same techniques used by the music videos.

Teenagers have their own ideas about what makes a good commercial. These are some features cited by teens in a 1994 poll.

The teens wanted commercials that had
- ✓ honesty
- ✓ humor
- ✓ a clear message
- ✓ originality
- ✓ good music that fits the commercial
- ✓ real attention-grabbing style
- ✓ a socially responsible theme.

A media study found that the average person sees and hears about 1600 advertisements a day. That includes print ads, billboards, radio commercials, and of course television commercials. You are probably an expert on the latest print ads and commercials.

1. In your opinion, what makes a good commercial? What elements should it have? Give examples from your experience.

_____

_____

_____

2. Vote for best commercial on a music television channel. Name the commercial and tell why you think it deserves to win.

_____

_____

_____

3. Which commercial is most popular among the people in your class? What features make it the winner?

_____

_____

_____

4. Describe some of the characteristics of your generation. What do you think advertisers would like to know about you?

_____

_____

_____

Lesson 3
The Power of Music Television

Music television is influential. It influences the way people dress and talk. It has influenced advertising on music and nonmusic channels. Most of all, it influences the sales of recordings. It can make someone a star almost overnight. It has even helped elect a president of the United States.

But is music television's influence good or bad? Some people argue that its influence is harmful. They say it turns teenagers into "vidiots." The chart on the next page shows comments for and against music television.

Good	Bad
Shows people of different racial groups.	Does not have enough ethnic representation.
Encourages teens to take politics seriously.	Shrinks viewers' attention span.
Improves communication among teens.	Has images that are too sexy.
Sets good models for teen and adult behavior.	Makes teens the slaves of advertisers.
Addresses important issues in today's society.	Prevents teens from thinking logically.

Choose any two statements. Tell whether you agree or disagree. Then support your point of view. Use what you know about music television. Use what you know about yourself and other teenagers. Give reasons and examples from your experience.

1. First Statement:

_____

_____

2. Second Statement:

_____

_____

3. Name one thing that has been influenced by music television. Tell what the influence has been. Tell whether you think the influence is good or bad. Explain why.

_____

_____

_____

_____

Plan a Music Video

Music videos are very creative productions. They involve teams of people. But often the idea for a video begins in one person's imagination. In this activity, you can work alone or with a group of classmates. Plan the story board for a music video. If you have a video camera, you can even record your production.

Prepare a script or outline of the video. Make a storyboard like the one above. A storyboard shows the main scenes in the video. Remember that most music videos are between 3 ½ and 5 minutes long.

Discuss these details before you begin.
- Choose a song that does not have a video or that has a video you'd like to change.
- Describe who is in the video. This might include singers, actors, friends, classmates, family members, and pets.
- Describe any make-up or props to be used in the video. How will people be dressed? How will they look? What will they need in order to carry out their part?
- In each storyboard screen, plan scenes or settings for each part of the song. Describe the settings on your storyboard. Tell what is happening in the scenes.
- Describe any special effects that will be used.
- Describe camera angles to be used.

Share your plan with other students.

Unit Test

Checking What You Have Learned

1. Each of the four phrases below could be used to complete the following
   statement. Circle the best choice. Then explain why you chose the answer you did.

   Music television channels
      a. play only music videos
      b. are influential media
      c. have only a few thousand viewers
      d. do not have commercials

   _____

2. Put an *X* next to the statements that are true. Explain why you judged the
   statements as you did.

   ❏ Recording companies and musicians are willing to change videos to meet a
   music channel's standards.

   ❏ Music videos are simple to make, and require only a few people.

   ❏ Audiences for music channels have an influence on advertisers.

   _____

3. Why are advertisers especially attracted to music television channels? Use examples
   and details to support your answer.

   _____

4. Some people claim that music videos are just advertisements for recordings. These
   people argue that the videos have no lasting value. What is your opinion? Answer
   the essay question on a separate sheet of paper. Support your answer with
   examples and details.

Checking How You Learned

Use the following questions to evaluate your performance in this unit.
   - What did you learn about music television channels that you did not know
     before?
   - Were you able to develop an argument for or against music television? If not,
     what information do you need in order to develop an argument?
   - How can you apply what you've learned in this unit as you watch music video

UNIT 3 Movies: The World of Illusion

You have your bucket of popcorn and a soft drink. You sit in a comfortable seat. The theater lights dim. The huge screen lights up, and the magic begins. With or without popcorn, audiences have been excited by movies for about 100 years. During this time, movies have changed from silent, jerky, black and white images. Today, they are laced with digital sound. They are wide-screened and full of dazzling color. Yet one effect has not changed in 100 years.

Movies still create an illusion. The illusion is that you are somewhere other than where you really are. You may be in another time in history. You may be somewhere in the future or deep in outer space. You may be in another town or country. You are seeing characters, images, and events that exist only on a screen in front of you. How does it happen?

Creating the Illusion

All movies have four stages of production. The first stage is the development stage. In the development stage, someone has an idea for a movie. The person may be a writer, director, producer, or talent agent.

In 1995, the average studio film cost $50 million to make.

109

Who Is Who in Movie Making.

Many people are involved in making a movie. These are just a few of them. To find out who helped make a movie, watch the credits at the end of the picture.

Producer: The person who oversees the whole movie. The producer hires the writer and director. The producer controls the business side of the movie.

Writer: The person who writes the script.

Director: The director is responsible for turning the script into a movie.

Editor: The person who puts the thousands of filmed shots together.

Director of Photography: The person who controls the cameras.

Casting Director: The person who hires the actors.

Effects Director: The person who is responsible for the special effects.

Actor's agent: A person who represents actors. The agent works to get roles and high fees for an actor.

Backer: A person or company that puts up money for the film.

After the idea, several things happen. A screen treatment and rough storyboard are prepared. Then a script is written. Money is raised. And the production is planned.

A screen treatment is an outline of the movie. It describes the characters, the plot, and the major scenes. It describes the theme and style of the movie. A rough storyboard is a set of drawings. The drawings show scenes from the movie. The treatment and storyboard help get studio executives and financial backers interested in the film.

After the treatment and storyboard are approved, a screenwriter writes a script. The script guides everyone working on the movie. It includes the words spoken by the actors. It describes the camera shots or angles. It describes costumes, scenes, and action.

At this stage actors and a movie crew are signed up.

The producer and director raise money to pay for the film. Most major films today cost tens of millions of dollars to make. The money may come from an entertainment company. It may come from a movie studio. It may come from backers. Money may come from a combination of sources.

Pre-Production

In the pre-production stage, the crew gets ready to shoot, or film, the movie. They make costumes and find or build locations where scenes will be shot. They design special makeup and plan special effects.

Production

At this stage, the scenes are filmed. Each scene may have many **shots.** A shot is a single camera **take.** In a take, the camera is turned on. It records the action. Then it is turned off.

Special effects are developed in the production stage. There are two kinds of special effects. **Mechanical special effects** can be shot in front of a camera. These might involve stunt actors, explosions, or crashes. Most special effects, however, are **optical special effects.** These include animated scenes. They include scenes using scale models and robots. They include images in which an object **morphs,** or changes, into another object. Optical special effects are created in a special effects studio. Most of them are designed and created on computers. The effects are added to the film in the post-production stage.

Post-Production

In the post production stage, the movie is put together from many pieces of film. The director, editor, and producer work together. They shape the film from thousands of takes. The editor can decide to mix scenes a certain way. The editor may use takes from a certain point of view to emphasize mood or action. The editor's choices shape the mood and pace of the movie.

At this stage the soundtrack is prepared. It includes music, dialogue, and other sounds.

After the movie is completed, it is **distributed.** To distribute a film means to get copies of it to theaters that will show it. Distribution depends on a movie's content and rating. A film cannot become a success unless it is widely distributed.

Camera Angles
There are eight basic camera shots. In a **pan** shot, the camera sweeps from right to left or left to right. In a **tilt** shot, the camera sweeps up and down or down and up. In a **dolly** shot, the camera glides toward or away from the subject. In a **tracking** shot the camera moves alongside a moving object. In a **boom** shot, the camera is on a crane and can move in any direction. In a **zoom** shot, the camera telescopes from far away to very close, or the reverse. In a **hand-held** shot, an operator holds the camera. This shot is used for some close-up action shots. An **aerial** shot is taken from a camera in a helicopter or airplane. These shots give you a sense of moving over a large area.

Film editing is one of the most creative roles in making a movie. The work is behind-the-scenes, but no job is more important.

Lesson 1
How Do Movie Makers Get You to Go to a Movie?

In the United States in 1995, there were about ten movie screens for every 100,000 people. That comes to about 25,000 screens. Americans spend about $5 billion a year on movie tickets. Yet many American movies make even more money from audiences in other countries. American comedy and adventure movies are very popular in Europe and Asia.

Advertising a movie is expensive. The cost of advertising a film can be as much as half the cost of making the film! For a movie that costs $30 million to produce, the makers may spend nearly $15 million to advertise it.

Movie makers choose from a wide variety of subjects. A movie maker's ideal subject is one that appeals to both younger and older audiences. Two examples are *Jurassic Park* and *Babe*.

The movies need you! Without viewers like you, movies could not exist. Yet you can't see *every* movie. Suppose you decide to see a certain movie. Do you know what influences helped you decide to see t*hat* movie?

Movie makers use several methods to try to get you into the theater. They begin by making a movie they think you'll want to see. The movie is also promoted and advertised.

A movie you'll want to see has one or more of these features:
- A known star—In 1995 two of the hottest stars were Jim Carrey and Demi Moore.
- A hot subject—In the 1970s and 1980s, martial arts subjects were big. In 1994 and 1995, movies about foolish or goofy characters were popular.
- A tie-in to something that is already popular—The tie-in might be with
    a popular video game such as *Mortal Kombat*

a television series, such as *Star Trek*
a popular book, such as *Jurassic Park*
a comic book character such as Superman or Batman
another movie with the same characters (a sequel)

In promoting or advertising a movie, movie makers use several methods:

- Trailers—This is a group of short clips from the movie. A trailer is shown in theaters before the movie is released. Trailers are also sometimes called "previews" or "coming attractions." The trailer contains some of the most exciting images from the film.
- Trailers on television channels—Trailers are often part of the commercials shown on cable and network stations.
- Advertisements on radio—Popular radio stations play audio trailers during commercial breaks.
- Posters and trailers in video rental stores—Some movies offer free take-home trailers on video cassettes. You may also see posters for new as well as old movies in your video store.
- Newspaper and magazine ads—These ads usually have photos or images from the movie. They also have quotations from reviewers who liked the movie. You have probably seen quotations such as "One of the year's 10 best!" and "Two Thumbs Up!"
- Sneak previews—An audience at a sneak preview gets to see two movies for the price of one. They see the movie they paid to see, then they get to see a new feature. A theater usually has a sneak preview for only one night. Movie makers hope that audiences will like the new movie and spread the word.
- Other influences—When a movie wins an award, the advertisers include this information in the movie ad. Some awards, such as Best Picture, draw more people to see the movie. Magazine and newspaper stories about movie stars also draw people to movies. Many people are also influenced by the reviews of a movie. Favorable television and print reviews can increase movie attendance.

1. Name a new movie you would like to see. What have you seen or heard that makes you want to see the movie?

_____

_____

_____

_____

Trailers may also come before the feature film on a video cassette. The trailer may be for a new movie or for another movie on video cassette.

The latest electronic movie ads are on the Internet. Some movie studios have home pages on the World Wide Web. You can dial up a site and download a trailer. See Part 4.

2. Some people do not like to see trailers when they go to a movie. They feel the trailers are like commercials on television. Some moviegoers feel they are forced to watch something they did not come to see. What is your opinion? Should trailers be shown before a feature movie? Give your reasons.

_____

_____

_____

_____

3. Which of the discussed methods do you think is the most powerful for getting people to see a movie? Explain your choice.

_____

_____

_____

_____

4. Suppose you were hired by a movie maker. What advice would you give about getting more people to go to a certain movie?

_____

_____

_____

_____

DISCUSSION

• •

In 1986, Bruce Willis was paid $5 million to make _Die Hard_. This was the most money any action star had ever been paid for a movie. In 1995, Jim Carrey was paid $20 million to make _Cable Guy_. Some big stars make one or two movies a year. While paying big bucks to stars, studios have sometimes lowered fees for ordinary actors. Do you think top stars are worth $10 million or even $20 million a picture? Discuss the pros and cons with your classmates.

Lesson 2
Evaluating Movies

A movie is much more than pictures on a screen. You have seen that it takes many skilled people to make a movie. A movie has many parts or elements. These include theme, plot, characters, acting, and direction. When you watch a movie, you can notice these elements. You can also evaluate them. You can tell whether you think they are good or bad and why.

These are some of the parts or elements in a movie.

Even if you do not like a movie, your evaluation helps you become a critical viewer. It helps you develop your ability to describe what you see and hear.

Theme	This is the big idea that the movie expresses. It reflects something about life. Some common movie themes are revenge, courage, love, justice, and the victory of good and evil.
Plot	This is the story the movie tells. It is the events that happen in the movie.
Characters	These are the people, animals, or objects that carry the action.
Acting	This is what the actors do. The actors should be convincing. They should make you believe they are the characters they are playing.
Direction	This is how the whole movie holds together. The movie should seem well thought out and well made.
Cinematography	This is how the movie looks on the screen. This is the job of the photography director.
Special Effects	These are actions or events that probably could not happen in real life.
Sound	This includes music as well as all other sounds.

Here are two reviews of the movie *Forrest Gump*. Each reviewer evaluates some of the elements of the movie. Yet, the reviewers have different opinions of the movie.

The Great Gump

by Janet James

You've gotta love *Forrest Gump*. As played by Tom Hanks, Forrest is an American hero. But he's a hero who can never understand how important he is.

The theme of the movie is America's rapid and amazing growth between the 1950s and the 1980s. In that growth, the movie suggests, the country lost its innocence. That innocence is Forrest Gump.

In the plot, Forrest is a sweet but limited boy in a man's body. He is swept along into every big event of the era, from the rise of Elvis to Watergate. Just by being a nice guy with a few tricks, he helps everyone. But what he really wants is to be reunited with his girlfriend.

Hanks's performance is great. He is tender and tough. Forrest may be stupid but he is lovable and wise. Hanks makes us feel these qualities.

The movie's main impact comes from the special effects. They're dazzling. Is Forrest really talking to President Kennedy? Is he really helping integrate the Alabama schools? It sure looks like it, even though we know it isn't true. Director Robert Zemeckis has shaped this movie with care. Yet he does not get in the way. He lets the actors and scenes work their magic. The soundtrack is a joy. How did they get those dead presidents to say those things? The songs are feel-good romance and pop. This movie is a must for everyone.

GUMP LUMP

by Rex Rich

The only thing that saves *Forrest Gump* is Tom Hanks. This hodgepodge of gimmicks is the latest from director Robert Zemeckis. The shaky theme is the naive hero in love.

The plot takes us through major events in American history between 1950 and 1980. Without trying, Gump finds himself at the center of every event. Well, so what? We know it isn't true. We know bad things happened then. And we know we can't change them. And we know that everyone loves someone who is out of reach.

I will say that the special effects are clever. Thanks to computers, Gump can meet and talk with dead presidents. He can play championship ping-pong and lead a football team to victory. This is entertaining, and Tom Hanks gives a winning performance. He doesn't play for laughs. His Gump is real, simple-minded, and likable. But after about an hour the tale gets boring. And you have two more hours to go! The director keeps the pace flowing, but that's not good enough. I'd like some real ideas to think about. And that soundtrack? It's music to snore by.

Describe a movie you have seen recently. Evaluate the elements from the movie. Then, on a separate sheet, write a review of the movie.

MOVIE _____

THEME _____

_____

PLOT _____

_____

_____

CHARACTERS _____

_____

_____

ACTING _____

_____

_____

DIRECTION _____

_____

_____

CINEMATOGRAPHY _____

_____

_____

SPECIAL EFFECTS _____

_____

_____

SETTING, COSTUMES, MAKE-UP _____

_____

_____

SOUND _____

_____

_____

Lesson 3
The Influence of Movies

MEDIA WISE

Most movies are rated. The rating helps parents decide if a movie is right for their children. A rating is based on the content of a movie. A ratings board considers a movie's theme. The board considers the language used in the movie. The board also considers such things as nudity, drug use, and violence. Then it gives the movie a rating. A "G" rating is for general audiences. It means the movie is appropriate for all ages. A "PG" rating means "parental guidance suggested." The movie may not be suitable for children. A "PG-13" rating means that some parts of the movie are not suitable for children under 13. An "R" rating means "restricted." A movie with this rating contains adult material. An "NC-17" rating means "no one under 17 admitted."

Movies have the power to change how people think and act. Right after the Vietnam War, Americans wanted to forget the war. It was a war America had lost. Americans did not want to honor the U.S. soldiers who fought in the war. Then, between 1977 and 1990, Hollywood made several movies about the war. During the same time, people's attitudes changed. They began to see Vietnam veterans as heroes. Congress passed bills to help the veterans. A memorial was built to honor soldiers killed in the war. It is likely that the Hollywod films helped influence the shift in attitude toward the Vietnam War.

This is just one example of the power of movies. In the case of the Vietnam War, the result was good or positive. Yet, many adults are concerned about the harmful effects movies may have. They believe violence in movies has a bad effect on young viewers. They believe some movies have unnecessary violence. But some movie makers say that moviegoers want violent films. After all, they say, many movies with violent content are big hits.

As you can see, there are different opinions about violence in movies. With your classmates, role-play a discussion about violence in movies. Choose one of three roles. One person is a parent of a teenager. One person is a Hollywood movie maker. One person is a teenager. Role-play for five minutes.

118

What is your personal opinion of violence in movies? Answer the questions below. Later, discuss your answers with your classmates.

1. Are some movies too violent? Give examples to support your opinion.

_____

_____

_____

_____

2. Why do you think violent films are popular?

_____

_____

_____

_____

3. Are violent movies bad for moviegoers? Why?

_____

_____

_____

_____

4. What might movie makers and movie viewers do in order to cut down on violence in movies?

_____

_____

_____

_____

5. Suppose Hollywood stopped making movies with a lot of violence. What do you think would happen?

_____

_____

_____

_____

An Idea for a Movie

Suppose you were a movie director, producer, or writer. What kind of movie would you like to make? Use the questions below to outline your movie.

1. What is the theme or topic of your movie?

_____

2. What is the plot of your movie?

_____

3. Who are the characters in your movie?

_____

4. What is the setting of your movie?

_____

Activity

On a separate sheet of paper, write a scene from your movie. Include dialogue that the characters will speak. Describe the characters' movements. Describe other events or actions. Share your scene with other students.

Unit Test

Checking What You Have Learned

State whether you agree or disagree with the following statement. Explain your reasons on the lines provided.

1. To promote a movie, movie makers advertise in only one medium.

   _____

   _____

2. Put an *X* next to the statements that are true. Explain why you judged the statements as you did.

   ❏ The soundtrack for a movie is prepared during the development stage.

   ❏ Whether an idea becomes a movie or not can depend on the screen treatment and storyboard.

   ❏ An ideal movie subject appeals only to one group of people, such as teens.

   _____

3. Why are movie makers willing to spend so much money to advertise a movie? Give examples to support your answer.

   _____

   _____

4. Compare a movie trailer to a written movie review. Which one might be a better choice in helping you decide to see a movie? Answer the essay question on a separate sheet of paper. Give examples to support your answer.

Checking How You Learned

Use the following questions to evaluate your performance in this unit.
- What did you learn about movies that you did not know before?
- Were you able to describe different elements of a movie? If not, how can you learn to recognize these elements?
- How can what you learned in this unit help you evaluate movies?

Programming TV Shows

Television and movies influence us in many ways. They send us messages about our world. As a critical thinker you must evaluate these messages and think carefully about what you see and hear. As a critical thinker, you can make up your own mind about issues.

In Unit 1, you learned about television. You learned what kinds of shows are popular. You examined the power of TV. You explored TV's strengths and weaknesses.

In Unit 2, you learned about music on TV. You looked at the features of music video channels. You explored music television's impact on viewers.

In Unit 3, you learned about movies. You explored how movies are made and sold. You examined their content and their influence.

Television is a business. Network executives try to fill their schedules with as many hit shows as they can. Hit shows mean more viewers. More viewers means more money from advertisers. Finding hits is not easy, though. No one can say for sure what shows viewers will like. In fact, nine out of ten shows do not even return for a second season.

For this project, you will do some TV programming. You will plan and schedule three hours of shows. You will also suggest commercials. Then you will share your ideas with the class.

STEP 1

Identifying the Time ....

Work in a small group. Choose a three-hour block of time. For instance, you might pick 8:00–11:00 Friday nights or 9:00–12:00 Saturday mornings.

Write your time block here: _____

Discuss the following questions. Write your conclusions.

- Who are the viewers likely to be during these hours? Adults? Teens? Kids?

  _____

- Do you think there will be an equal number of men and women? Why?

  _____

- Do you think the audience will change as time passes? If so, how?

  _____

STEP 2

Planning the Time ••••••••••••••••••

Discuss how you want to break up the block of time. For example, you might have six half-hour shows. Or, you might have four half-hour shows and one one-hour show. You should have at least four shows.

▶ Create a programming schedule. Here is an example:

Schedule: 7:00–10:00 Monday Nights

7:00–7:30   Show #1: 30 minutes

7:30–8:00   Show #2: 30 minutes

8:00–8:30   Show #3: 30 minutes

8:30–9:00   Show #4: 30 minutes

9:00–9:30   Show #5: 60 minutes
9:30–10:00

Schedule:

_____

_____

_____

_____

_____

◀ Use this box for your programming schedule. Number the shows.

Planning the Shows ·········

Work as a group to plan the shows for your schedule. Brainstorm possibilities. Share and discuss ideas. Consider the likely audience for each show. Plan shows that will appeal to that audience. Use your imagination. Here is an example:

SHOW #1 (time slot: 7:00-7:30): This is a half-hour game show called *Teen Trivia*. Teams of teens compete. They answer questions about topics of interest to teens.

Describe each of your shows on the lines that follow. Use separate sheets of paper if you need more space.

SHOW #1 (time slot: _____):

_____

SHOW #2 (time slot: _____):

_____

SHOW #3 (time slot: _____):

_____

SHOW #4 (time slot: _____):

_____

SHOW #5 (time slot: _____):

_____

SHOW #6 (time slot: _____):

_____

STEP 4   Planning Commercials...

Suggest one commercial for each time slot. Tell why the commercial would be a good choice. Here is an example:

TIME SLOT: 7:00-7:30. A commercial for acne cream would be a good choice. The game show *Teen Trivia* will draw teen viewers. Teens buy many acne products.

Time slot: _____

_____

_____

Time slot: _____

_____

_____

Time slot: _____

_____

_____

Time slot: _____

_____

_____

Time slot: _____

_____

_____

Time slot: _____

_____

_____

STEP 5

Evaluating the TV Schedules...

Present your programming schedule to the class. Discuss each of the other groups' schedules. Talk over the following questions.

- Is the three-hour block of time divided well?
- Are the shows likely to be hits?
- Are the shows good choices for their time slots?
- Are the suggested commercials good choices for their time slots?

PART 4

FOCUS ON COMPUTER-BASED MEDIA

The first electronic computer was as big as a small house. It was built in 1949 and was called ENIAC. The letters stand for Electrical Numerical Integrator and Computer. The computer had 18,000 glass tubes, like light bulbs. The tubes got hot and often blew out causing the computer to break down. The first computer was unreliable and inefficient.

SOFTWARE AND HARDWARE Computers have come a long way since ENIAC. Today, powerful computers are the size of a textbook. Modern computers run thousands of programs, or **software.** Software lets the computer do specific tasks. With the right software, you can write letters, do math, or play games. **Hardware** is any electronic or mechanical device that runs software. Computers are hardware.

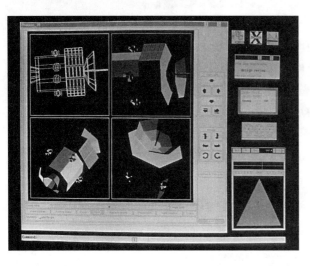

Some software comes in a **multi-media** format. Multi-media combines sound, text, and images. Images may be photos or moving pictures like those on TV.

AUDIENCE In 1993, about 26 percent of the homes in the United States had a computer. Nearly half of all home and school computer users are under 18.

Many thousands of computers around the world are linked to one another. They form **networks.** Each computer in the network contains a huge amount of information on many subjects. So networks contain vast amounts of information. The collection of all world-wide networks make up the **Internet.**

Computer users can connect to the Internet through a **modem.** A modem lets a computer send and receive information over phone lines.

MARKET Computer hardware and software are not paid for by advertising dollars. Instead, people buy hardware and software directly from the makers. In 1994, Americans bought $8 billion in personal computers.

Hardware and software makers advertise mostly in print media. Some companies have also begun to advertise on the Internet. These advertisers expect sales over the Internet to grow in the future.

IMPACT Computers have had a great impact in America and other countries. Thousands of products, from toys to machines, are controlled by computers. Most U.S. businesses depend on computers to carry out daily tasks. Computers also provide huge amounts of information to the public.

Yet computers also have drawbacks. One study found that computer users use more paper, not less. Many people object to the violence of some video games and the "anything-goes" content on the Internet.

CRITICAL ISSUES One issue surrounding computers is access. Access applies to who does and does not get to use computers. Not everyone can afford hardware and software. Many schools cannot afford computers. Yet at least half of all jobs in America require workers to have computer skills. Educators and businesses worry about the gap between computer "haves" and "have nots."

In Part 4, we will explore different kinds of software. We will also examine features of the Internet.

Playing and Learning with Multimedia

Here are four articles from a teen magazine on multimedia products. Read the articles. How do they compare to what you already know about multimedia products?

Build a City from Your CD-ROM

This week we are reviewing a CD-ROM game that you are sure to want to try. For now, forget about arcade-type fighting games. Those are fun, but you do not learn much about the real world. The CD-ROM that we looked at is Maxis's SimCity. In this program, you build a city from the ground up. Sound boring? Not at all! You will have many problems to solve, many obstacles to overcome, and many different ways of looking at how a city develops. You will plan housing for different income groups. You will decide on the best locations for airports, fire stations, and parks. What will you do about pollution and its impact on life in your city? Will you raise property taxes to pay for schools and education? You will have lots of challenging decisions to make. This may not be more fun than Killer Instinct, but you will learn more. After you spend time with this CD, you may want to run for mayor.

▶ A CD-ROM disk is a small plastic disk like a music CD. The letters "CD-ROM" stand for Compact Disk Read Only Memory. A CD-ROM disk contains software in a multimedia format. A CD-ROM player plays CD-ROM disks. The multimedia images show up on a computer screen. Sound comes through speakers in the player or in the computer.

More Zap and Zip!

▶ American teens spend $6 billion on arcade games a year. That's a lot of quarters! Why are these games so popular?

For arcade game fans, several collections are available on CD-ROM now. One that we saw is called Atomic Arcade. This set includes twelve games that are described as "zapping, zinging, and outrageously funky." You can be the judge for about $10. This is just one of many CD game collections that will keep you zapping for hours.

128

An Exciting Trek Through an Encyclopedia

How would you like to be taken on a trip by Captain Jean-Luc Picard of the Starship Enterprise? You are in the passenger seat with Compton's new Interactive Encyclopedia.

Captain Picard (actor Patrick Stewart), takes you on a tour of endless excitement found in a CD-ROM encyclopedia. You do not have to turn any pages. Just follow Captain Picard and click on words and pictures that you would like to explore. You will find video clips, graphics, text, and sound. Are you doing a research paper on whales? The CD-ROM encyclopedia lets you hear whales, see whales swimming, see a map showing their migration, and learn many facts about their habitat and life. You can make your own presentation by copying parts of the encyclopedia article to a floppy disk.

> Most CD-ROMs are **interactive.** The user makes some kind of action that has an effect on the screen. The player may use a "joy stick" or a **mouse.** Both are devices that change a player's hand movements into movements on the screen. Screens also have **hypertext.** These are words you click on that take you to related subjects.

An Educational CD-ROM

Would you like to learn Spanish? Try Pro-One's Multimedia Spanish. This CD-ROM uses multimedia to help you learn vocabulary and grammar. Hear the sounds, see the words, and see what the words describe. Like most educational CDs, you learn at your own speed. Spend as much time as you need on verbs, nouns, and sentences. And have fun while you are learning.

Lesson 1
Hooked on the Games? Evaluate!

Video games can be addictive. Here is a story about someone who got hooked.

It all started with a new video game I got two weeks ago. I thought I could break the habit, but I was hooked. The first night, I played for an hour. Then three hours the next night. Then five hours. Then more. I could tell things were bad when the police broke down my bedroom door. My parents had called them. Mom and Dad hadn't seen me in 24 hours.

"What have you been doing all day?" Dad demanded.

"Didn't you hear us calling you?" Mom asked, wringing her hands. "Why was your door locked? We were worried about you."

Then they saw my computer glowing in the darkened room, and they knew. "Those games, again!" Mom said, shaking her head. "I don't understand it. You've got to stop. You're ruining your life."

They don't understand. I'm so close to breaking the spell. Once I do that, I'll have another clue to unlock the mystery. I know I can do it.

The story is exaggerated, of course. Yet many people—especially teenagers—spend hours a day playing video games. Are the games worth it? To answer this question, you need to analyze the games you play. Evaluate them in relation to cost, time spent, entertainment value, and educational value. The questionnaire below will help you.

Video Game Evaluation Sheet

Name of game: _____

Cost of the game: to rent _____ to buy _____

How much time do you spend a week playing the game? _____hours

What effect does the game have on your life? Consider these questions: Does it cut down on the time you spend studying? Does it cut down on the time you spend with friends and family? Does it affect your sleep? Does it affect your eating habits? Does it affect your ability to concentrate on other things?

_____

_____

_____

_____

How would you rate the game's graphics? Consider these ideas: How interesting is the game to look at? What special effects are there, if any? How clear are the images?

_____

_____

_____

_____

How would you rate the game's sound? Consider these ideas: Is the music appropriate to the game? Are voices appropriate to the content of the game? Are voices respectful toward players? Are they exciting or humorous? Are they easy to understand?

_____

_____

_____

_____

Many video game packages have a rating. The rating is like those used for movies. The ratings indicate the appropriate audience for the games. For example, a rating "KA" is for kids to adults, ages 6 and up. A rating "T" is for teenagers, ages 13 and up; a rating "M" is for mature individuals, 17 years old and older. A rating "A" is for adults only.

Media Wise

Some video games improve players' reflexes or hand-eye coordination. Some games go beyond this to build thinking and memory skills. A few games require players to keep careful notes about details, evidence, and decisions. Some games involve a player's **intuition**—the ability to form a hunch and follow through on it. These skills are useful for purposes besides playing video games.

How would you rate the level of difficulty? Easy? Moderately difficult? Very difficult? Explain your choice.

_____

_____

_____

What is the game's educational value? Consider this question: What do you learn?

_____

_____

_____

What is the game's entertainment value? Consider these questions: How do you feel after you have played for a while? Is it easy to stop playing? Do you hate to stop? What makes you want to keep playing? Do you play with others or talk about the game with others?

_____

_____

_____

Do you think playing this game is a good way to spend your time? Why?

_____

_____

_____

DISCUSSION

Some video games are **spinoffs** of movies. When a movie has been a big success, video game makers buy the rights to use the name of the movie and sometimes even pictures or voices of the stars. In the 1990s, Hollywood began making movies based on successful video games. A curious thing happens, however. Games based on movies do not make as much money as the movies made. Movies based on games usually don't become hit movies. Why do you suppose this happens?

Lesson 2
A Diskful of Knowledge

There is plenty of information for you on CD-ROMs. One group of CDs is called informational, or reference, CDs. These include encyclopedias, dictionaries, atlases, and almanacs. They have much of the information you need to prepare reports or explore any subject. Here is a brief description of the major kinds of informational CDs.

Media Wise

One CD-ROM disk holds the equivalent of 250,000 typewritten pages. One disk can hold almost all of the information from a twenty-one volume set of encyclopedias.

- CD-ROM encyclopedias have all the topics you would find in a print encyclopedia. Several CD-ROM encyclopedias also are multimedia. They have animation, moving video images, and sound.

- With a CD-ROM dictionary, you type in a word. The definition pops up on the screen. If you misspell the word, the dictionary will show you possible choices of what the word might be.

- A CD-ROM atlas contains many kinds of maps. It may also give population data, charts, and graphs. Some atlases have state songs, flags, flowers, and gems. Some even show aerial video clips of places.

- A CD-ROM almanac puts thousands of facts at your fingertips. Just type in a topic or name. The almanac brings information to the screen.

Of course, informational CD-ROMs are not perfect. You may find that for some projects you need other sources. These are some of the pros and cons of CD-ROMS.

Pros	Cons
• CDs are less expensive than books. A CD-ROM encyclopedia costs about $100. A set of print encyclopedias costs $700 or more. • CD-ROM has multimedia. Video clips and sound can give you information that you can not get in a printed book. • A CD-ROM disk takes up a small amount of space. However, do not forget the space it may take up in your computer! • Finding information on a CD-ROM is usually faster than finding it in a book. Just click and point.	• Informational CD-ROMs need to be updated. A yearly update for an encyclopedia can cost $50 or more. • CD-ROM equipment is expensive. You need a computer plus equipment that plays a CD-ROM. This can cost $1000 or more. • Books usually contain more printed information. Print encyclopedia articles are longer than articles on a CD-ROM. • Computers can crash. Books do not. Also, you can read books during a power failure.

What other pros and cons can you think of?

_____

_____

Look at the list of topics below. Assume you are writing a two-page report on each topic. Use what you know about CD-ROMs, books, newspapers, and magazines. Decide which one would be best for looking up information on the topic. Explain.your choices.

• The mythical animal called a unicorn

_____

• The history of the guitar

_____

• A biography of writer Maya Angelou

_____

• A current problem in Buenos Aires, Argentina

_____

Lesson 3
My Teacher: The Computer and the CD-ROM

"I think I learn more and I learn faster than I did before I used a computer."

"I like it because it's interactive—I have control. It goes at my pace."

"It's easy to talk to. I don't feel embarrassed if I make a mistake."

"I'm a visual learner. The pictures help me."

"My test scores have gone way up."

These comments were made by students who have been using educational software. Educational software is designed to teach certain subjects and skills. These include mathematics, reading, foreign languages, science, and social studies. Many educational software products are available on CD-ROM.

Educational software is interactive software. You can input words or numbers. You may even speak to the computer if the software recognizes voices. The software gives you feedback. It may tell you that your answers are right or wrong. It may give you hints. It may take you to another level of difficulty. Some software even gives rewards, such as short games.

In 1993, 62 percent of elementary school teachers had computers in their classrooms. Forty-four percent of high school teachers had them. Do you think the percentages will increase in the future? Why?

These are some additional benefits of using educational software.

BENEFITS

- Virtual reality software presents lifelike situations. Virtual reality images seem real but they are not.
- Students focus on their work. There are fewer behavior problems in the classroom.
- Students do more useful talking with each other and with the teacher.

- Computers can give students a great deal of information in a short time.
- Students feel more responsible for their work.
- Students feel more confident.

Would educational software be a good teacher of *any* subject? Read the subjects below. Use what you know about the subject and about computers. Tell whether the subject is a good one to learn by computer. Explain your answer.

- The human brain

_____

_____

- How to swim

_____

_____

- The history of Vietnam

_____

_____

Your Opinion

What subject would you like to study by using educational software? Tell why you think this would be a good way to learn a subject.

_____

_____

_____

New York University has a Virtual College. Sitting at home with a computer, students take courses. They receive multimedia lectures. They exchange electronic mail with other students and with the teacher. They get reading materials and have discussions by computer. Each course costs $2000. Do you think junior high and high schools will become like this in the future? Why or why not?

Your CD-ROM Wish List

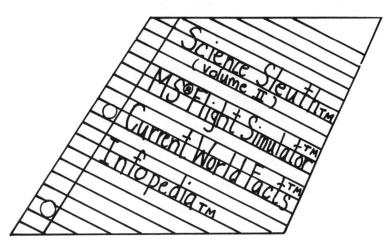

There are hundreds of CD-ROMs of all kinds—entertaining, informational, and educational. In this activity, you will make a list of ten CD-ROMs you would like to have. You can list ones that really exist. Or you can list ones you would like to see created.

Use separate sheets of paper for your work. Follow these steps:

- Decide what categories of CD-ROMs you would like to have and how many you would like in each category. For example, you may want two games, four informational, and four educational.

- Describe the qualities you would like to see in each CD-ROM. These could be features such as hypertext and 3-D graphics. Refer to the descriptions in the Unit Opener on pages 128–129 if you need help.

- Get a catalog of CD-ROMs. You can order one from any mail-order software company. Ask your local computer store. You might also read reviews of software in computer magazines.

- Compare contents and prices.

- Describe how you would use each CD-ROM. Explain the benefits you expect to gain from each one.

- Share your list with your classmates. Which are the most popular categories of CDs? Which are the most popular titles?

Unit Test

Checking What You Have Learned

1. Put an *X* next to the statements that are true. Explain why you judged the statements as you did.

   ❏ Video games are a major form of entertainment in America.

   ❏ Video games are not as popular as movies.

   ❏ Using a video game is not as expensive as going to see a movie.

   _____

   _____

2. Why might someone buy a CD-ROM encyclopedia instead of a set of encyclopedias? Use examples and details to support your answer.

   _____

   _____

3. What important things have you learned about computers and CD-ROMs that you can use when you think about learning subjects or skills in the future? Use examples and details to support your answer.

   _____

   _____

4. Some people claim that computers are just too complicated, expensive, and impersonal. These critics would rather stick with print media, broadcast media, and the telephone. What is your opinion of advantages and disadvantages of computers and CD-ROM software? Answer the essay question on a separate sheet of paper. Support your answer with examples and details.

Checking How You Learned

Use the following questions to evaluate your performance in this unit.
* What did you learn about CD-ROMs that you did not know before?
* Were you able to develop criteria for evaluating a CD-ROM game? If not, what can you do to create these criteria?
* How can you apply what you've learned in this unit to your use of computers and CD-ROM products?

Your Guide to the Internet

You have heard the *buzz* (talk), but do you know the scene? Have you *surfed* (explored) the *Net* (Internet)? Each day, millions of people "plug in" their computers to a huge database of information. The database offers movie reviews, sports scores, even magazine articles. Users can send and receive electronic "mail." Sound amazing? Welcome to the information superhighway!

As of the spring of 1995, between 30 and 40 million people in 160 countries around the world had access to the Internet.

What Is the Internet?

The **Internet** is a world-wide connection of thousands of computers. The computers are linked into groups, or **networks,** called **hubs.** These networks are connected by phone systems and communications satellites. The Internet is really a network of networks.

The word **cyberspace** describes the vast interconnections among computers and other electronic equipment. It includes equipment that needs to be plugged in. It also includes equipment that does not, such as cellular phones and satellites. Some people think cyberspace is identical to the Internet. Others view the Internet as part of cyberspace.

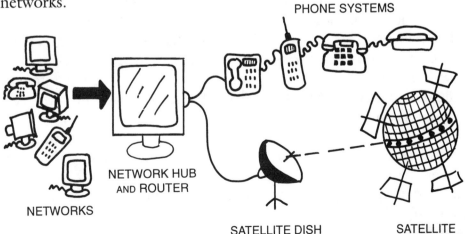

PHONE SYSTEMS

NETWORK HUB AND ROUTER

NETWORKS

SATELLITE DISH

SATELLITE

What Do You Need to Get onto the Net?

Ask about the Internet at your local library. Many libraries have computers with Internet connections. Your school may also have a computer with the Internet. Community centers and local businesses may also have Internet links.

To get onto the Internet, you need the following items:
- Computer. ($800 and up)
- Modem–a device that lets your computer send and receive information over the phone system. A modem allows you to be **"on-line"** with another computer. ($100 and up)
- Software–a computer program to connect you to an on-line service that links with the Internet. (usually free)
- A credit card to pay monthly fees charged by an on-line service that connects you to the Internet. (Basic monthly fees are about $10. You will be charged more for Internet use.)
- A telephone line that you can expect to use for an hour or more at a time. (You may have conflicts if there are other phone users in your home.)
- Money to pay your phone bills, which will increase with Internet use.

The staff at a computer store can tell you what equipment you will need and how to hook it up.

How Do You Connect to the Internet?

You get onto the Internet through an on-line service. To use an on-line service, you need a modem. The service will send you software to install on your computer. Then you sign on to the service. You will see a menu listing several features of the service, such as "Reference," "Entertainment," or "News." The menu will also include "Internet" as a choice. Some on-line servers just connect you to the Internet. Two of these systems are PPP (Point-to-Point Protocol) and Dial-Up Access. They do not have all the features that other services have. But they may cost less per month.

Once you are connected to the Internet, you can use **menus** to find information. These are lists of topics offered by the on-line services. You can also **download,** or copy, software that will help you find information at Internet sites. Some on-line systems select popular Internet sites that you can explore. Just use your mouse to point and click.

Using the Internet takes time. So many people use the Internet that phone lines get jammed. Sometimes getting to an Internet site can take several minutes. Getting information and images from the site can take even more time. Busy sites are like busy phone lines. You have to keep trying. Be careful! Before you know it, you will have spent hours on the Net.

The three biggest on-line servers as of the summer of 1995 are America On Line, Compuserve, and Prodigy. Microsoft has just entered the field. AT&T and MCI have plans to enter. These companies know that the Internet will be big business in the future.

Lesson 1
Using the Net

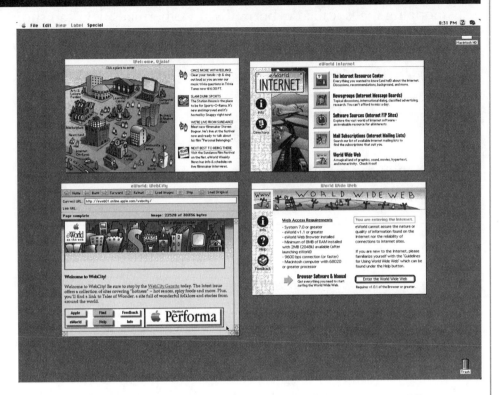

A world of information and entertainment opens to Net users. Here are some Net features you may want to try:

- **E-mail** or **electronic mail**—You can exchange messages with computer users anywhere in the world. Of course, the other users must be connected to the Internet.
- The **World Wide Web** (WWW)—This is a huge collection of electronic "pages". Web pages include words, pictures, and sometimes sounds. They may deal with nearly any subject. The Web organizes and presents some of the best information on the Internet. Some on-line servers offer a menu of "cool" sites. Web pages are created by companies, groups, and individuals. To use the Web, you will need special software, called a Web Browser. You can usually download or copy this free from an on-line service.
- **Usenet newsgroups**—These are on-line chat or discussion groups. Each group has a special topic. You chat with others in the group by typing comments. Your comments appear on the computer screen. People can share information and ideas with others interested in the same topic.
- Entertainment software—To download software, you use an Internet feature called **FTP** (File Transfer Protocol). To learn

As of the summer of 1995, there were already about 3.5 million documents or pages on the WWW. About 6,000 new pages are added daily. There are pages on many topics. Some offer jobs. Some advertise services. Some are electronic magazines or "Webzines."

Think twice before giving credit card information over the Internet. Buying products this way is new. Your card information may not be protected well. Your card number may be stolen by **hackers.** Your card may be charged for things you did not buy.

what is available, you will need other software such as Gopher or Veronica. These help you search for software and information on specific topics.

- Shopping—If you have a credit card, you can order items such as brownies or ballet tickets. The latest trend is computer shopping malls, called **cybermalls.** In cybermalls, you can shop by category: books, outdoor equipment, food, and so on.

How Would You Use the Internet?

Now that you know about the Internet, think about how you might use it. If you have already used the Internet, describe your experiences. Use the following questions as a guide.

1. Where might you find a computer that you can use to explore the Internet?

_____

_____

_____

_____

2. What two features of the Internet would you most like to use? Why?

_____

_____

_____

_____

3. Describe two subjects that interest you. Which Internet features do you think would help you learn more about these subjects?

_____

_____

_____

_____

4. Describe other ways in which the Internet could be useful to you.

_____

_____

_____

_____

Lesson 2
Evaluating What You Get from the Net

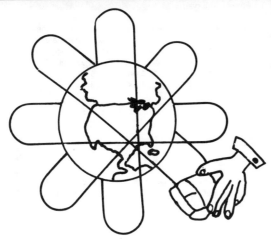

The Internet is a huge democracy. Anyone can join the Internet. Anyone can compose e-mail and create files of information. Anyone can create a web page and post messages on a bulletin board for others to read. People are free to say whatever they like. As of 1995, there has been no censorship.

Remember that millions of people use the Internet. They have many different interests and ideas. Some of the information on the Net is good, reliable information. But some of it is not. You may find information that is out of date, misleading, biased, or just plain wrong. How can you tell the good from the bad?

Here are some guidelines:

- Decide whether what you are reading is fact or opinion. Remember that facts can be checked. Opinions are just beliefs. You can get both facts and opinions on the Net. Just be careful not to confuse the two.

- Consider the source. Individuals and organizations can be unreliable. Look for evidence that a person knows what he or she is talking about. Does the person have credentials? Does the person have experience related to the topic? Do you recognize the name of the organization? Does someone you trust know the organization?

- Check other sources on the Internet. You can find information in many ways on the Internet. Suppose you get information from someone in a newsgroup. You can double-check the information by posting a question in a related newsgroup. Or you can check another source, such as an on-line almanac, encyclopedia, or another data base.

Some parts of the Internet may not be available to you. This depends on the on-line service you use to connect to the Net. Some services give you only parts of the Net. Others give you the whole Net. The Net is so vast, you may never know the difference.

◄ On the Internet, you are pretty much anonymous. You may use your real name, but many people use a "screen" name or nickname. No one sees what you look like. You control your identity. You might find yourself chatting with another teenager. You might also be chatting with an astronaut, one of your favorite singers, a professor, or your next-door neighbor. People get to know you only by what you say and how you say it.

Read these two bulletin board messages. Then answer the questions.

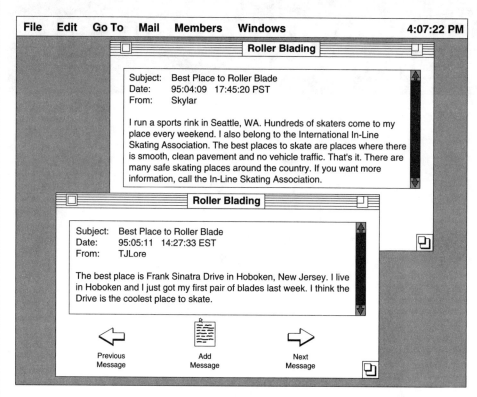

1. Why would you have reason to doubt TJLore's suggestion?

_____

2. How could you get another opinion if you wanted it?

_____

3. What evidence suggests that Skylar's information may be good?

_____

4. What topics could you look under to get additional information?

_____

_____

_____

5. Describe a time when you checked a fact in a second source. What was the topic? What did you find out?

_____

_____

_____

Lesson 3
Interview with a Net User

You may not have had a chance to use the Internet yourself. But you probably know someone who has. This could be a relative, friend, classmate, teacher, or librarian. It could be someone at a local business.

Even if you have not used the Net yourself, you know enough now to ask questions about it. You can use your questions to find out more about the Net. To do so, you will interview someone who has used the Net.

You can interview in person, on the phone, or by mail. Maybe you have a computer and an on-line service. In that case, you can post your questions to an on-line bulletin board. You can also interview someone in an Internet forum.

Use the questions below to conduct your interview. Add other questions of your own. Use a separate sheet of paper if you need to.

1. How much time do you spend on the Internet?
   _____ hrs per day, week, or month

2. What is your favorite site? Why?

   _____

   _____

3. What are two other sites you like? What is special about them?

   _____

   _____

About 19 million people in North America are on-line. Americans access the Internet through computers in homes, businesses, high schools, colleges, libraries, and other organizations. The number of on-line users is growing daily.

4. What is the most useful thing you've learned on the Net?

_____

_____

5. How has using the Internet affected your life?

_____

_____

Additional questions:

_____

_____

_____

_____

_____

_____

_____

_____

_____

_____

_____

_____

DISCUSSION

The Internet is worldwide. Yet the language of the Internet is almost entirely English. Many people in foreign countries do not speak English. They are not able to take advantage of the many resources the Internet offers. It is true that the Internet was developed in America by English-speaking people. Some Americans argue that English should be the language of the Internet. Is this fair? Discuss whether or not English should be the main language of the Internet.

A Road Map to the Internet

Are you ready to go on-line and use the Internet? Use the tips and ideas in this activity. They can help you get onto the Net and have fun.

- Start by visiting your school library or computer center. Ask to use a computer that has an Internet connection. Ask the librarian or person in charge to help you.

- First you'll need to connect to an on-line service. The computer may already be set up on-line. Ask the person in charge if you are not sure.

- Choose the Internet from the on-line menu. You may see another menu that gives you choices such as "World Wide Web," "Web Browser," "Net Launcher," "WAIS (Wide Area Information Service)," and "FTP (File Transfer Protocol)." Choose one and follow the instructions on the screen. You will probably be asked to enter the name of a topic or the address of a web site. Choose a topic that you are interested in. Key in the word and see what happens. All Web sites have a universal resource locator or URL. This is a specific address. It is a string of letters and symbols such as http://www.tvnet.com/UTVL/utvl.html, which is the address for the Ultimate TV List.

- Here are some topics you might try:

  - Key in the name of your favorite sports team, such as the Red Sox.
  - Find a review of *Forrest Gump* or another movie. Try the Internet Movie Database. Its URL is http://www.msstate.edu/movies/
  - Find the Internet "Cool Site of the Day" by keying http://www.infi.net/cool.html
  - Find sports statistics by typing ESPNet SportsZone. The URL is http://espnet.sportszone.com/

  - Would you like a multimedia tour of the solar system? Key The Nine Planets at http://seds.lpl.arizona.edu/nineplanets/nineplanets/nineplanets.html
  - Use a web tool such as Gopher, Veronica, or Archie to look up information on any topic.

After you've found information, record it or print it out. Make a list of the sites you visited, then share your information with your classmates.

Unit Test

Checking What You Have Learned

1. Circle the best choice to complete the statement. Then explain why you chose the answer you did.

   The Internet is

   a. like a city's telephone system

   b. only a place to do electronic shopping

   c. a network of networks

   d. only for hackers

   _____

2. Put an *X* next to the statements that are true. Explain why you judged the statements as you did.

   ❑ Access to the Internet can be costly.

   ❑ Access to the Internet is free.

   ❑ If you don't own a computer, you can still get access to the Internet.

   _____

3. What strategies can you use to decide if information from the net is believable or useful? Use examples to explain your answer.

   _____

4. Why is the Internet an important tool for students to learn to use? Answer the essay question on a separate sheet of paper. Support your answer with examples and details.

Checking How You Learned

Use the following questions to help you evaluate your performance in this unit.
   - What did you learn about the Internet that you did not know before?
   - Were you able to describe ways that you would use the Internet? If not, how could you figure out ways to use the Internet?
   - How can you use what you have learned to gain access to the Internet?

Advertising On-Line

It may be a fad. Then again, it may be the biggest change in advertising since television. It is advertising on-line. Hundreds of products are now advertised on-line. They range from T-shirts to multimillion-dollar movies. Some companies are paying as much as $200,000 to have ads designed for on-line audiences. What is different about advertising on-line? Here are some facts:

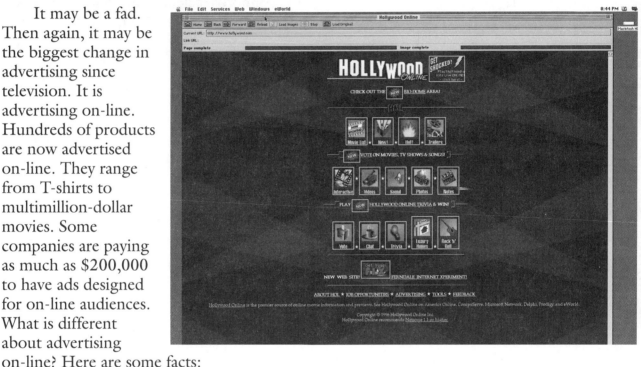

- Millions of people connect on-line. They are all potential buyers.

- As of the summer of 1995, the demographics for on-line users are not clear. Some reports say that most users are 18 to 40 years old with money to spend. Other reports are more cautious.

- Rather than miss the boat, companies are rushing to advertise. Advertising on-line will be just as competitive as advertising in other media.

- It is unlikely that on-line advertising will replace advertising in other media. On-line services are nothing like the Super Bowl. Millions of users do not tune into the same site at once. Companies see on-line advertising as just another way to reach buyers.

- On-line advertising is different, however. Remember that on-line communication is interactive. Users make the choices. So ads are set up to get users to click and find out more about a product. For example, an advertisement for a new movie may offer games, sound clips, or pictures from the movie. It may allow users to download a preview of the movie. It may allow users to send e-mail to the stars of the movie. But the user makes the choices. If the advertising pages are not interesting, the user will just click off to another site.

- On-line buyers are already buying. They use credit cards to buy things like books, software, outdoor gear, and packaged foods.

- On-line users generally dislike advertisements on e-mail. E-mail is an on-line area that users want to keep free of ads. Even so, some people post ads such as "$100,000 in 30 days."

- On-line advertisers use some of the same techniques they use in other media. These are some of them:

  - Free premiums, such as a free CD recording

  - Claims of savings for users who buy on-line

  - Entertaining features such as photos, celebrity interviews, contests, and trivia quizzes

Answer the following questions about advertising on-line.

1. What difficulties do you think on-line advertisers face?

_____

_____

_____

2. What are some of the advantages of on-line advertising?

_____

_____

_____

ACTIVITY: Work with a group of your classmates. Choose a product to advertise on-line. Plan how you would present the ad to on-line users. Describe the features you'd use to keep people interested.

Creating a Web Page

The computer has brought about a revolution. It has brought a totally new way of creating, using, and communicating information. Computer use is now world-wide. Modern daily life in many countries would be impossible without the computer. In Part 4 of *Media Today,* you have explored two major applications of computer technology.

In Unit 1, you learned about interactive multimedia programs available on CD-ROM. These programs fall into three categories: entertainment, information, and education. They include games, encyclopedias, and how-to programs. Games are fun, but you need to evaluate whether or not they are worth your time and money. Even though education and information programs are dazzling, they are not always the best choice for some tasks.

In Unit 2, you learned about the worldwide network of networks, the Internet. People use the Net for many different purposes. It gives users enormous amounts of information. It also allows large numbers of people to connect with each other and to express ideas and opinions.

For this project, you will work with a small group of students. You will design a World Wide Web page for the Internet. You will choose themes or topics that are important to you. You will decide how your page will look and what links it will have to other themes and topics. Then, you will present your page to the class.

STEP 1

Brainstorm Ideas for the Page......

What will your page be about? Use the graphic organizer on the next page to list possible topics. There are Web pages on hundreds of topics. Topics include hobbies, sports, news, music, personal advice. Narrow the topic for your page. Suppose you choose sports as the general topic. Choose a specific sport, such as hockey or basketball. Then break this topic into subtopics, such as NBA players, scores, and championship games.

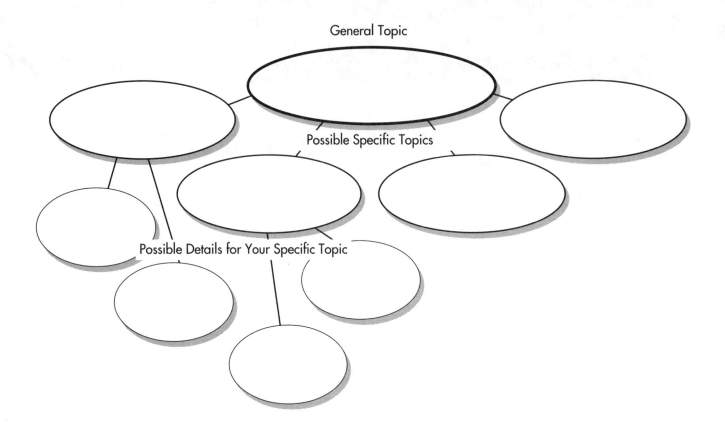

General Topic

Possible Specific Topics

Possible Details for Your Specific Topic

The following screen is the beginning of a web page.

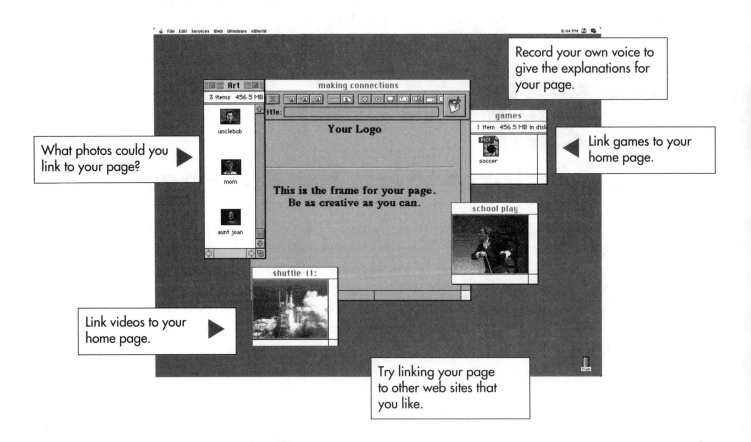

Record your own voice to give the explanations for your page.

What photos could you link to your page?

Link games to your home page.

Link videos to your home page.

Try linking your page to other web sites that you like.

Write a Draft Introduction to Your Page......

STEP 2

The introduction includes a greeting to users. Then it describes what your page is about. In a paragraph, tell users what they can expect from your page. You may want to wait until you plan your links (Step 3) before you write the final version of your introduction.

_____

_____

_____

STEP 3

Plan the Links for Your Page......

A Web page provides hypertext links to other information. Underlined words and icons (small pictures) represent hypertext. A user can click the mouse on one of these and get more information about the underlined words or topic. For example, under NBA Stars, you might have a hypertext link that says "Interviews with the stars," or "Vital statistics on the stars." A user would click on this hypertext and be linked to interviews or statistics. A web page usually has at least six of these links. Remember that the linked information could lead to sounds, pictures, text, or even videos. Use the graphic organizer below to plan your links. You may need to do some research to get more information about your topic.

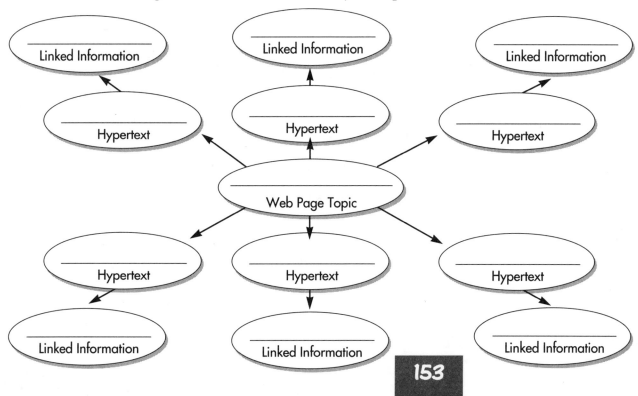

STEP 4

Prepare and Present the Results..............................

Use a separate sheet of paper to display the final design for your Web page. Type the text or use a word processor. Use colored pencils, inks, or paint to create the icons. Give your page a title and design a page logo. The logo is a graphic symbol that represents your page.

When your page is complete, present it to the class. In presenting your page, follow these steps:

* Describe the topic and content of the page.

* Describe the links. Tell why you created these specific links.

* Tell what benefit you think users will get from your page.

* Ask for questions and comments about your page.

STEP 5

Evaluate Your Page..............

Compare the Web pages from different groups. Use a simple score card like the one below for each group. Assign 1 or 2 points for each question. Give a total of 10 points for a perfect score.

Did the introduction make me want to use the page?   _____

Were the subtopics clear and interesting?   _____

Were the links clear and interesting?   _____

Was the logo clever and unique?   _____

Were the icons appropriate?   _____

Total Score: _____

GLOSSARY

advertorial   an advertisement section in a magazine that looks like an article or a feature (p. 22)

biased   slanted toward one viewpoint (p. 47)

broadcast medium   medium such as radio or television that sends electronic signals through the air; some television is not broadcast but is sent through cables (p. 36)

CD-ROM   a compact disc that contains software in a multimedia format (p. 133)

censor   to ban certain material from newspapers, films, books, or other media (p. 13)

column   an article in which a writer, or columnist, gives an opinion on a topic (p. 14)

commercial   an advertisement that is presented on television, radio, or film (p. 64)

controversial   causing argument or objections among many people; violent images are an example of a controversial element in the media (p. 71)

credibility   characteristics that make someone or something believable or reliable (p. 47)

criterion   (plural: **criteria**) a set of rules, standards, or tests used to make a judgment about something (p. 60)

cyberspace   the electronic environment created by the links among computers and other electronic equipment such as satellites (p. 139)

demographics   characteristics of a population including age, interests, and income level; magazines and other media study the demographics of their audience (p. 21)

documentary   factual film about a particular subject

download   to transmit or copy information or a software program to a computer from an on-line source (p. 140)

editor   person whose job is to make decisions about what is published in a newspaper or magazine (p. 20)

editorial   a newspaper or magazine article that gives the editor's or owner's opinion (p. 14)

episode   one show of a television series (p. 84)

freelance writers   writers who sell articles to many different magazines instead of working for one magazine (p. 19)

general interest magazine   a magazine that tries to appeal to many different kinds of readers (p. 18)

hard news   factual accounts of important events (p. 8)

hardware   the electronic, mechanical, and magnetic devices of a computer (p. 126)

hidden agenda   the unstated reasons that a person or company has for doing something (p. 47)

hub   a computer network (p. 139)

human-interest story   a story that focuses on the human side of news and often appeals to readers' emotions (p. 8)

hypertext   on a CD-ROM, words that can be used to bring related subjects up on the screen (p. 129)

infomercials   television commercials that look like factual programming; some infomercials are as long as full-length TV programs (p. 98)

interactive   able to be affected or changed by something the user does; most CD-ROMs are interactive (p. 129)

Internet   the interconnected computers

155

around the world, capable of communicating with one another (p. 139)

mainstream newspaper a newspaper that stresses straightforward, fact-based news articles (p. 11)

mass media media such as television, radio, and newspapers that can reach a large group of people (p. 1)

media (singular: medium) methods by which information can be communicated to people over a distance; television and newspapers are forms of media (p. 1)

media literacy an understanding of media methods and messages (p. 3)

modem a device that allows a computer to send and receive information over the telephone (p. 140)

multimedia able to combine such elements as sound, text, photographs, and moving video images (p. 126)

network 1. a system of many computers connected together (p. 139); 2. a company that distributes programs to television channels (p. 84)

on-line connected to the Internet (p. 140)

op-ed page (so named because it is usually opposite the editorial page) a page in a newspaper that contains columns, articles, letters from readers, and other items expressing opinions (p. 14)

pilot a sample show of a television series (p. 85)

playlist the songs played by a radio station (p. 74)

prime time most popular time to watch TV—the evening hours between 8 p.m. (7 p.m. on Sundays) and 11 p.m. (p. 84)

product placement a way that advertisers display products as part of the scenery or story line of TV shows or movies (p. 93)

propaganda information and opinions that are intended to convince people to accept or reject a certain idea (p. 54)

ratings statistics that show the size of a radio or television audience (p. 84)

rhetorical question a question to which no answer is expected (p. 31)

soft news stories that are interesting but less important than hard news stories; soft news includes interviews, editorials, and film reviews (p. 8)

software the instructions or programs that tell a computer what to do (p. 126)

special-interest magazine a magazine that targets only certain readers, such as those who share an interest or belong to a particular age group (p. 18)

spin-off a television show or video game based on ideas or characters from another source (p. 132)

stereotype an oversimplified, predictable way of showing a character, as on a TV show or in a movie (p. 87)

tabloid a newspaper that stresses dramatic stories, often about sensational subjects (p. 11)

target audience a specific group of people that media producers or advertisers want to reach (p. 23)

virtual reality a computer-created world that seems very real (p. 136)

World Wide Web large directory of information on the Internet (p. 141)